Contents

List of resources	3
Introduction	4
How to use the CD-ROM	5

Improving the environment in the UK PAGE 7
Notes on the CD-ROM resources	8
Notes on the photocopiable pages	14
Photocopiable pages	15

Global citizenship and sustainable development PAGE 19
Notes on the CD-ROM resources	20
Notes on the photocopiable pages	27
Photocopiable pages	30

Settlements PAGE 37
Notes on the CD-ROM resources	38
Notes on the photocopiable pages	48
Photocopiable pages	50

Contrasting localities in India PAGE 54
Notes on the CD-ROM resources	55
Notes on the photocopiable pages	62
Photocopiable pages	64

A European locality: the Tyrol PAGE 68
Notes on the CD-ROM resources	69
Notes on the photocopiable pages	77
Photocopiable pages	78

Licence
IMPORTANT – PERMITTED USE AND WARNINGS – READ CAREFULLY BEFORE USING

Copyright in the software contained in this CD-ROM and in its accompanying material belongs to Scholastic Limited. All rights reserved. © Scholastic Ltd, 2005.

The material contained on this CD-ROM may only be used in the context for which it was intended in *Ready Resources*. School site use is permitted only within the school of the purchaser of the book and CD-ROM. Permission to download images is given for purchasers only and not for borrowers from any lending service. Any further use of the material contravenes Scholastic Ltd's copyright and that of other rights holders.

Save for these purposes, or as expressly authorised in the accompanying materials, the software may not be copied, reproduced, used, sold, licensed, transferred, exchanged, hired, or exported in whole or in part or in any manner or form without the prior written consent of Scholastic Ltd. Any such unauthorised use or activities are prohibited and may give rise to civil liabilities and criminal prosecutions.

This CD-ROM has been tested for viruses at all stages of its production. However, we recommend that you run virus-checking software on your computer systems at all times. Scholastic Ltd cannot accept any responsibility for any loss, disruption or damage to your data or your computer system that may occur as a result of using either the CD-ROM or the data held on it.

IF YOU ACCEPT THE ABOVE CONDITIONS YOU MAY PROCEED TO USE THIS CD-ROM

Text © Tony Pickford and Heather Swainston
© 2005 Scholastic Ltd

Published by Scholastic Ltd, Villiers House,
Clarendon Avenue, Leamington Spa,
Warwickshire CV32 5PR

Printed by Bell & Bain Ltd, Glasgow

234567890 678901234

British Library Cataloguing-in-Publication Data
A catalogue record for this book is available from the British Library.

ISBN 0-439-96488-1
ISBN 978-0439-96488-3

Visit our website at
www.scholastic.co.uk

CD developed in association with
Footmark Media Ltd

Authors
Tony Pickford
and Heather Swainston

Editor
Tracy Kewley

Project Editor
Wendy Tse

Assistant Editors
Aileen Lalor and Kim Vernon

Series Designer
Joy Monkhouse

Designer
Catherine Mason

Cover photographs
© DigitalVision/Getty Images

Acknowledgements

Extracts from the National Curriculum for England © Crown copyright material is reproduced with the permission of the Controller of HMSO and the Queen's Printer for Scotland.
Extracts from Programmes of Study from The National Curriculum reproduced under the terms of HMSO Guidance Note 8. © Qualifications and Curriculum Authority.

The Day Chocolate Company for the use of text and illustration of 'Riyayatu's Story' interview © 2002, The Day Chocolate Company (previously unpublished). **Guardian Newspapers Ltd** for the use of an abridged article 'Fight to the last resort as Alpine crisis looms' by Robin McKie which first appeared in *The Observer*, 19 September 2004 © 2004, Guardian Newspapers Limited, 2004. **Oxfam** for the use of the extracts 'What is Global Citizenship?' and 'Seven key concepts of sustainable development (Panel for Education for sustainable development, 1999) from *Global Citizenship: The Handbook for Primary Teachers* by Mary Young and Eilish Commins © 2002, Oxfam (2002, Chris Kington Publishing and Oxfam Publishing. **The Penguin Group (UK)** for the use of 'The British, serve 60 million' from *Wicked World!* by Benjamin Zephaniah © 2000, Benjamin Zephaniah (2000, Puffin). **Teachers In Development Education (TIDE)** for the use of an extract from the Development Compass Rose/TIDE Consultation Pack ©1995, Development Education Centre (Birmingham) Tide Centre, Birmingham.

Due to the nature of the web, the publisher cannot guarantee the content or links of any of the websites referred to. It is the responsibility of the reader to assess the suitability of websites.

The rights of Tony Pickford and Heather Swainston to be identified as the authors of this work have been asserted by them in accordance with the Copyright, Designs and Patents Act 1988.

All rights reserved. This book is sold subject to the condition that it shall not, by way of trade or otherwise, be lent, hired out or otherwise circulated without the publisher's prior consent in any form of binding or cover other than that in which it is published and without a similar condition, including this condition, being imposed upon the subsequent purchaser.

No part of this publication may be reproduced, stored in a retrieval system, or transmitted, in any form or by any means, electronic, mechanical, photocopying, recording or otherwise, without the prior permission of the publisher. This book remains copyright, although permission is granted to copy pages where indicated for classroom distribution and use only in the school which has purchased the book and in accordance with the CLA licensing agreement. Photocopying permission is given only for purchasers and not for borrowers of books from any lending service.

Made with Macromedia, a trademark of Macromedia, Inc. ®
Copyright © 1984–2000 Macromedia, Inc.

Minimum Specifications:
PC: Windows 98 SE or higher
Processor: Pentium 2 (or equivalent) 400 MHz
RAM: 128 Mb
CD-ROM drive: 48x (52x preferred)

MAC: OS 9.2 (OSX preferred)
Processor: G3 400 MHz
RAM: 128 Mb
CD-ROM drive: 48x (52x preferred)

List of Resources on the CD-ROM

The page numbers refer to the teachers' notes provided in this book.

Improving the environment in the UK

Rural school, Rural school grounds, Urban school, Urban school grounds	8
Cars	9
Walking bus	9
Cycling	9
Eco-Schools	10
Recycling, Composting	10
Before school ground changes, After school ground changes	11
Litter-picking, Planting	12
Public gardens	12
School council	13
Videos: Noise in classroom, Noise outside classroom, Dinner hall	13

Global citizenship and sustainable development

Multicultural group, Looking at the world	20
Peter's Projection world map	21
Bicycle, Bicycle lane	22
Train	22
Metro	22
Rush hour in India, Rickshaw	22
Kingsmead School, Photovoltaic panels	23
Solar panel in Morocco	24
The Fairtrade Mark, Fair trade products	24
Map of Africa	25
Cocoa pod on tree, Cutting pods down, Cutting pods open, Fermenting beans, Drying beans, Weighing beans, Processing chocolate in factory, Chocolate sold in shops	25
UK farmers' market	27
Thai floating market	27

Settlements

UK map	38
Animation: Settlement hierarchy	38
OS map of the Lake District	39
Farm	39
Hamlet	40
Hawkshead village: view 1, view 2, view 3	41
Small town	41
Market town	42
City centre street	43
Manchester – urban renewal	44
Conurbation	44
Defensive site	45
OS map of Kelso, Kelso Town Hall	46
Place names	47

Contrasting localities in India

Map of India	55
Climate chart: Two Indian locations	55
Market in Kerala	56
Source of the River Ganges	57
Tiger in Kanha National Park	57
Gateway of India in Mumbai	58
Street in India, Video: Indian traffic	59
Video: Rush hour in India	59
Tropical beach	60
Railway station	61
Deforestation	61

A European locality: the Tyrol

Map of Austria	69
Tyrolean farmhouse	69
Modern alm, Traditional alm	70
Alpine cows	70
Cutting grass	71
Gondola leaving base, Gondola on mountain, Gondola station	71
Gondola in winter	72
Söll in summer	73
Street in Söll	73
Primary school in Söll	73
Grossglockner and glacier	74
Mountain refuge	75
Video: Panorama of Innsbruck	75
Climate chart: Innsbruck and Manchester	76
Video: Alps from the air	76

Image © Karen Robinson

Image © Tony Pickford

INTRODUCTION

This book and CD-ROM support the teaching and learning set out in the QCA Scheme of Work for geography in Years 3 to 6 (Key Stage 2). The CD provides a large bank of resources – both visual and aural. The book provides teachers' notes, which offer background information, ideas for discussion and activities to accompany the CD resources. There are also photocopiable pages to support the teaching. All have been specifically chosen to meet the requirements for resources listed in the QCA units for Years 3 to 6 (Key Stage 2). Some additional resources and ideas have also been included to enable teachers to develop and broaden these areas of study if they wish. These include activity sheets to help children clarify their thinking or to record what they find out.

The resources and activities are not intended to provide a structure for teaching in themselves, but are designed to give a basis for discussion and activities which focus on the knowledge, skills and understanding required by the National Curriculum for geography. The children are encouraged to develop such key skills as observing, questioning, describing, sorting and sequencing.

Graphicacy is one of the key skills in geography and it covers all forms of pictorial communication of spatial information: ground-level photographs, oblique and vertical aerial photographs, diagrams, signs and symbols, and maps of all sorts – from pictorial to Ordnance Survey. Maps and their conventional use of plan view are important in geography, but children see their world from eye-level. There is a large conceptual leap between eye-level and plan (aerial) view, and children can be helped to make sense of, and understand, the relationship between horizontal and vertical viewpoints by the use of intermediate perspectives, that is, views taken from a range of oblique angles.

Links with other subjects

Literacy
There are a number of close links between the units covered in this book and work on literacy. The discussion activities contribute directly to the requirements for speaking and listening. There is considerable opportunity for the children to develop their independent writing skills as they produce reports or write captions using the word cards. Images from the CD could be printed to stimulate independent writing, or to illustrate it.

Maths
Skills such as counting, measuring, matching, ordering and sequencing are essential to both geography and maths. Children develop skills in analysing and interpreting graphs through the use of comparative climate charts.

Science
The discussion of land use and geographical locations enables children to appreciate the variety of landscapes to be found in both their own and contrasting areas.

Citizenship
In the chapter on global citizenship, children develop a greater awareness of their place within a diverse world. There are also opportunities to think of ways of improving the immediate and wider environment through recycling, the use of public transport and effective waste management.

ICT
Children are encouraged to use the internet whenever possible to search for more information on subjects they are studying.

HOW TO USE THE CD-ROM

Windows NT users
If you use Windows NT you may see the following error message: 'The procedure entry point Process32First could not be located in the dynamic link library KERNEL32.dll'. Click on **OK** and the CD will autorun with no further problems.

Setting up your computer for optimal use
On opening, the CD will alert you if changes are needed in order to operate the CD at its optimal use. There are three changes you may be advised to make:

Viewing resources at their maximum screen size
To see images at their maximum screen size, your screen display needs to be set to 800 x 600 pixels. In order to adjust your screen size you will need to **Quit** the program.

If using a PC, open the **Control Panel**. Select **Display** and then **Settings**. Adjust the **Desktop Area** to 800 x 600 pixels. Click on **OK** and then restart the program.

If using a Mac, from the **Apple** menu select **Control Panels** and then **Monitors** to adjust the screen size.

Adobe Acrobat Reader
To print high-quality versions of images and to view and print the photocopiable pages on the CD you need **Adobe Acrobat Reader** installed on your computer. If you do not have it installed already, a version is provided on the CD. To install this version **Quit** the 'Ready Resources' program.

If using a PC, right-click on the **Start** menu on your desktop and choose **Explore**. Click on the + sign to the left of the CD drive entitled 'Ready Resources' and open the folder called 'Acrobat Reader Installer'. Run the program contained in this folder to install **Adobe Acrobat Reader**.

If using a Mac, double-click on the 'Ready Resources' icon on the desktop and on the 'Acrobat Reader Installer' folder. Run the program contained in this folder to install **Adobe Acrobat Reader**.

PLEASE NOTE: If you do not have **Adobe Acrobat Reader** installed, you will not be able to print high-quality versions of images, or to view or print photocopiable pages (although these are provided in this book and can be photocopied).

It is recommended that certain images, such as maps and aerial views, are viewed and printed in **Adobe Acrobat Reader** as it will be easier to focus on specific areas.

QuickTime
In order to view the videos and listen to the audio on this CD you will need to have **QuickTime version 5 or later** installed on your computer. If you do not have it installed already or have an older version of QuickTime, the latest version can be downloaded at http://www.apple.com/quicktime/download/win.html. If you choose to install this version, **Quit** the 'Ready Resources' program.

PLEASE NOTE: If you do not have **QuickTime** installed you will be unable to view the films.

Menu screen
▶ Click on the **Resource Gallery** of your choice to view the resources available under that topic.
▶ Click on **Complete Resource Gallery** to view all the resources available on the CD.
▶ Click on **Photocopiable Resources** (PDF format) to view a list of the photocopiables provided in this book.
▶ **Back:** click to return to the **opening screen**. Click **Continue** to move to the **Menu screen**.
▶ **Quit:** click **Quit** to close the menu program and progress to the **Quit screen**. If you quit from the **Quit screen** you will exit the CD. If you do not quit you will return to the **Menu screen**.

Resource Galleries
▶ **Help:** click **Help** to find support on accessing and using images.
▶ **Back to menu:** click here to return to the **Menu screen**.
▶ **Quit:** click here to move to the **Quit screen** – see **Quit** above.

Viewing images
Small versions of each image are shown in the Resource Gallery. Click and drag the slider on the slide bar to scroll through the images in the Resource Gallery, or click on the arrows to move the images frame by frame. Roll the pointer over an image to see the caption.
▶ Click on an image to view the screen-sized version of it.
▶ To return to the Resource Gallery click on **Back to Resource Gallery**.

Viewing videos
Click on the video icon of your choice in the Resource Gallery. In order to view the videos on this CD, you will need to have **QuickTime** installed on your computer (see 'Setting up your computer for optimal use' above).

Once at the video screen, use the buttons on the bottom of the video screen to operate the video. The slide bar can be used for a fast forward and rewind. To return to the Resource Gallery click on **Back to Resource Gallery**.

Listening to sound recordings
Click on the required sound icon. Use the buttons or the slide bar to hear the sound. A transcript will be displayed on the viewing screen where appropriate. To return to the Resource Gallery, click on **Back to Resource Gallery**.

Printing
Click on the image to view it (see 'Viewing images' above). There are two print options:

Print using Acrobat enables you to print a high-quality version of an image. Choosing this option means that the image will open as a read-only page in **Adobe Acrobat** and in order to access these files you will need to have already installed **Adobe Acrobat Reader** on your computer (see 'Setting up your computer for optimal use' above). To print the selected resource, select **File** and then **Print**. Once you have printed the resource **minimise** or **close** the Adobe screen using — or **X** in the top right-hand corner of the screen. Return to the Resource Gallery by clicking on **Back to Resource Gallery**.

Simple print enables you to print a lower quality version of the image without the need to use **Adobe Acrobat Reader**. Select the image and click on the **Simple print** option. After printing, click on **Back to Resource Gallery**.

Slideshow presentation
If you would like to present a number of resources without having to return to the Resource Gallery and select a new image each time, you can compile a slideshow. Click on the + tabs at the top of each image in the Resource Gallery you would like to include in your presentation (pictures, sound and video can be included). It is important that you click on the images in the order in which you would like to view them (a number will appear on each tab to confirm the order). If you would like to change the order, click on **Clear slideshow** and begin again. Once you have selected your images – up to a maximum of 20 – click on **Play slideshow** and you will be presented with the first of your selected resources. To move to the next selection in your slideshow click on **Next slide**, to see a previous resource click on **Previous slide**. You can end your slideshow presentation at any time by clicking on **Resource Gallery**. Your slideshow selection will remain selected until you **Clear slideshow** or return to the **Menu screen**.

Viewing on an interactive whiteboard or data projector
Resources can be viewed directly from the CD. To make viewing easier for a whole class, use a large monitor, data projector or interactive whiteboard. For group, paired or individual work, the resources can be viewed from the computer screen.

Photocopiable resources (PDF format)
To view or print a photocopiable resource page, click on the required title in the list and the page will open as a read-only page in **Adobe Acrobat**. In order to access these files you will need to have already installed **Adobe Acrobat Reader** on your computer (see 'Setting up your computer for optimal use' above). To print the selected resource select **File** and then **Print**. Once you have printed the resource **minimise** or **close** the Adobe screen using — or **X** in the top right-hand corner of the screen. This will take you back to the list of PDF files. To return to the **Menu screen**, click on **Back**.

IMPROVING THE ENVIRONMENT IN THE UK

Content and skills
This chapter links to Unit 8 of the QCA Scheme of Work for geography at Key Stage 2, 'Improving the environment', and encourages children to think about their own environment and the people who live and work there. It focuses on children using the school buildings, grounds and immediate locality to investigate environmental issues and improvements. It also reinforces and extends their knowledge and understanding of the wider world and encourages them to develop respect for human and natural diversity and take responsibility for their actions. The National Curriculum recognises that sustainable development is both one of the purposes of education and an explicit part of its values.

The teachers' notes contain background information about the resources and include ways of using them as a whole class, for group work or as individuals. Some of the activities link with other areas of the curriculum, such as RE, citizenship and PSHE. Wherever possible, the activities encourage the children to ask questions and develop an enquiring approach to their learning.

Resources on the CD-ROM
Among the resources on the CD, there are photographs of school buildings and grounds in rural and urban areas. There is a selection of photographs depicting transport to school including children being dropped off at school, a walking bus and children cycling to school. There is also a picture of the Eco-Schools flag. Ways of improving the environment are illustrated by pictures of bottle banks and composting, as well as by 'before' and 'after' views of changes to a school building and grounds. Pictures of children using litter pickers and planting, and an image showing the local council playing its part, illustrate further ways of helping the environment. A photograph of a school council meeting shows ways in which children can have a role in improving their school environment. Finally, there is a short video which highlights the issue of noise in schools.

Photocopiable pages
The photocopiable pages in the book are also provided in PDF format on the CD-ROM and can be printed from there. They include:
- word cards containing essential vocabulary for the unit
- an 'environmental action tree' activity sheet
- a sheet for children to record the rubbish that they throw away.

Geographical skills
Using the resources and activities in this chapter will develop children's ability to read and interpret photographs and to identify key features within visual images. The activities also support the development of geographical vocabulary.

Image © Learning through Landscapes

NOTES ON THE CD-ROM RESOURCES

SCHOOL BUILDINGS AND GROUNDS

Rural school, Rural school grounds, Urban school, Urban school grounds

The photographs show schools and school grounds in rural and urban areas of the United Kingdom. The contrasts are quite stark, although the similarities in terms of the functions of the spaces and some of the environmental issues are similar. The school grounds are an excellent place to start exploring the local area and for finding ways for the children to become involved in improving the environment. Children will be familiar with their own school building and grounds and will be able to suggest ways in which the location and design will affect their experience of school and its impact on the local and wider environment. Practical fieldwork observations can easily be made within the immediate locality. The key geographical ideas of place, space and the environment can all be developed in the school grounds. The rural school is an older building surrounded by large fields and open countryside. The urban school is on three levels surrounded by streets and houses in a highly populated area. The playing area is all concrete compared to the open spaces of the rural school.

Discussing the photographs
▶ Remind the children of the number of different environments in your local area and that schools around the country are situated in very different environments. Show the pictures to the children and point out that two relate to a rural area and the other two are in an urban environment.
▶ Ask the children what they think the surrounding environment is like for the schools in the images.
▶ Ask the children to think about what the different environmental problems in and around the two schools might be.
▶ Point out that even though the schools look different, they will also have some of the same issues to address, such as transport to school, litter, recycling and play areas.
▶ Encourage the children to think about the different environmental problems in and around their own school.
▶ Ask the children to consider the advantages and disadvantages of being in a rural or urban school.

Activities
▶ Ask the children to imagine that they are describing your school to a child in another country who has asked what the school environment is like. Look around the school and at the school grounds and, working in small groups, ask the children to make a list of issues to bring back to the classroom to share.
▶ As a class, discuss the environmental issues that you have at your school. Make a list of the problems and discuss possible solutions.
▶ Draw a plan of the school and grounds. Mark the environmental issues on the maps. Discuss with the children the location of the different issues highlighted. Do they all occur in the same area?
▶ Decide who is responsible for the problems and for the solutions and develop an environmental charter for the school.
▶ Ask the children to imagine what your school and the schools in the photographs will look like in ten or twenty years' time. Discuss what the environmental issues might be in the future.
▶ Set the children the task of finding a newspaper or magazine story focusing on an environmental issue. Consider what connections this has to the environmental issues identified in school.
▶ Put a collection of books about environmental issues and stories about the environment in the book corner. Ask the children to bring in things made out of recycled materials. The schools library service or local development education centre may have collections of artefacts from overseas that include recycled items – for example, flip-flops made out of recycled tyres.

IMPROVING THE ENVIRONMENT IN THE UK

▶ Invite a representative from an environmental organisation into school to talk about what they do to protect and improve the environment.
▶ Challenge the children to design an environmental quiz including subjects such as recycling, energy, transport and ideas for taking action.

TRAVELLING TO SCHOOL

Cars

Many children travel to school by car. For some, this is unavoidable because of parents having to continue on to work but for others it may be an unnecessary car journey. The number of cars travelling to schools is a problem, especially in the morning when the school run coincides with rush-hour traffic. Slow-moving and stationary traffic causes an increase in fuel consumption and exhaust fumes and this has a negative effect on the environment. It also presents a danger to children crossing roads and affects people who live in the vicinity.

Walking bus

The school children in this picture are taking part in a school walking bus. This is a system where children are collected along the bus route and are walked to school in a group. They are being supervised by a teacher and a classroom assistant. They are all wearing reflective jackets to make them highly visible to traffic. This system will have reduced the number of car journeys made to school and will help to cut down on congestion outside school. It is also a very healthy and safer alternative for the children.

Cycling

The Safe Routes to School initiative is a project which aims to provide a safer road network in the vicinity of schools and to promote cycling, walking and public transport use among school children. Children need to be very safety-conscious when cycling and should always wear a helmet and reflective clothing and have lights on their bikes if they are cycling in the dark. Cycle ways, traffic signs, crossing facilities and cycle parking also make cycling safer.

Discussing the photographs
▶ Look at each photograph in turn and identify the different ways in which children are travelling to school.
▶ Find out what is the most popular form of transport in your class for travelling to school.
▶ Ask the children what they think are the advantages and disadvantages of each mode of transport shown in the photographs.
▶ Discuss the pollution and health issues of each form of transport for individuals and for the environment. For example, cycling is a good way of keeping fit and is pollution-free.
▶ Have the children always travelled to school in the same way? If not, what made them change?
▶ Discuss how the practicalities of travelling to school may be different in rural and urban areas.

Activities
▶ Conduct a travel-to-school survey throughout the whole school.
▶ If you do not run a walking bus, discuss with the children how the school might go about planning this.
▶ Investigate different modes of transport and routes around the school area including cars, buses, roads, footpaths and cycle lanes.
▶ Plan how children and families could reduce their own use of unsustainable transport.
▶ Make a school travel plan – how could it be easier and safer to walk or cycle to school?
▶ Take the issue to the school council if you have one and write a policy to promote walking and cycling and link this to writing an environmental charter for the school.
▶ Invite a local road safety officer to come and talk about road safety and perhaps to arrange for cycle safety lessons.

IMPROVING THE ENVIRONMENT IN THE UK

- Hold a school assembly about ways of travelling to school and the different effects this has on the environment.
- Ask the children to write captions for the photographs to either persuade or discourage people from using that form of transport.
- Set up a role-play activity to explore issues about travelling to school.

SCHOOL AND THE ENVIRONMENT

Eco-Schools

Eco-Schools is an international environmental education programme for school. It is run by the Federation for Environmental Education and managed by ENCAMS (Environmental Campaigns) in the UK. The Eco-Schools programme supports schools in improving their environmental management and sustainable development through an effective citizenship process and whole school involvement. It focuses on education and direct action, encouraging children to take practical steps in reducing the school's impact on the environment. The programme involves an eco-committee that takes an active role in carrying out an environmental review and implementing an action plan for the school. It provides an excellent framework for promoting whole school involvement (children, teachers and other staff) and work with the local community, thus raising awareness and respect for the environment beyond the limits of the school grounds. This programme promotes the children's sense of responsibility for their immediate environment and engages them in important decision-making processes.

The programme began in 1994 based on the principle that young people should be involved in local environmental and sustainable development – a need that was highlighted at the UN Conference on Environment and Development in 1992. Currently about 12,000 schools are participating in the programme in 30 countries in Europe, Africa and South America. The Eco-Schools Green Flag is the top international accolade awarded to schools with a high level of achievement in their programme and it is a respected eco-label for environmental education and performance. More information can be found at www.eco-schools.org.uk.

Discussing the photographs
- Remind the children about what sustainability is. Ask them to give you some examples.
- Tell the children about the Eco-Schools initiative.
- Ask the children if they think their school is an environmentally friendly school.
- What do the children think they would have to change in their school in order for it to be an eco-school?

Activities
- Design an eco-audit of the school or ask the local authority to send someone in to undertake this.
- Ask the children to walk around the school on a fact-finding tour to see what the environmental issues are.
- Invite the children to put forward their ideas about what a very environmentally friendly school would be like.
- Working in groups, ask the children to think about what improvements could be made to the school environment. Make a collage of their drawings and pictures from magazines.
- Challenge the children to design an eco-game to raise awareness about the issues – for example, a quiz or board game about environmental issues in the school and/or around the world.

Recycling, Composting

The management of household waste is usually shared between the District and County Councils. For example, in Cheshire the collection of household waste lies with the District Councils and disposal with the County Council. The majority of councils provide recycling schemes (although this is not statutory) and many offer compost bins. Many recycling points are provided in easily accessible locations such as supermarket car parks. Materials that can be recycled in household waste are: glass; paper; cardboard; cans (drink and tin cans) and plastic. Everybody needs to play a part in reducing waste and reusing and recycling as much

IMPROVING THE ENVIRONMENT IN THE UK

as possible. It also makes sense to try to reduce the waste we produce. We can, for example, buy to last, think about what we are buying when we shop, compost garden and kitchen waste and stop junk mail.

Discussing the photographs
▶ Discuss what the children in the picture are doing.
▶ Ask the children if they recycle anything at home. Have they got a 'green bin' or a recycling collection in their locality?
▶ Show them the picture of the recycling bins. Have the children seen these in their locality, for example in supermarket car parks?
▶ Show them the boy with the composting bin and explain what a composting bin does. Suggest one item that can be composted, for example coffee grindings, then ask the children what other compostable items they can think of. Tell the children that garden and vegetable waste takes up about one quarter of the waste in our bins but this could be used to make compost. It is simple to do, benefits the garden and slims your bin.

Activities
▶ Consider the environmental issues in your classroom, rather than on a school scale. Ask the children to list everything that is thrown away in a day in their classroom.
▶ Collect all the rubbish each day for a week, then weigh it and sort it into different types. Discuss which types of rubbish could be recycled and how this would be done. For example, could it be done on site or would it have to be taken away from the school?
▶ The children could set up a recycling scheme and see how much they can recycle in a month. They could use different-coloured bins for different types of rubbish.
▶ Discuss what the children think about the amount of waste they have produced. Make some decisions about how this waste is going to be reduced. For example: buy to last, buy unpackaged produce, buy refills for soap dispensers or fabric conditioner bottles, reuse plastic bags or boxes.
▶ Ask the children to find out more about organisations working with people to reduce waste. Examples include Waste Watch (www.wastewatch.org.uk) and Friends of the Earth (www.foe.co.uk).
▶ Ask the children to think of things they have at school and home that they no longer use. Write a list of all the ways such items could be reused. Consider holding a 'Reuse fair'.
▶ Find out about waste management and recycling in other countries. In a number of African countries, for example, tyres are recycled into flip-flops and bicycle brakes and in Dhaka (Bangladesh), plastic bags have been banned because of the harmful effect they are having on the environment.
▶ Hold a debate about the advantages and disadvantages of plastic bags for the environment and consider the alternatives. Discuss and decide what arguments you would use to try and persuade people to buy and use a canvas bag instead of plastic bags.
▶ Visit the website of Tools for Self Reliance, a charity that recycles tools, at www.tfsr.org.
▶ Use some reclaimed materials to make collages or a junk orchestra.

Before school ground changes, After school ground changes

These pictures show Danleigh Primary School in Inverness, Scotland. The school took part in a project called Start Growing Upwards, which aimed to bring growth and greenery into otherwise dismal school grounds. The building in the background on the left-hand side of the picture is not part of the school. The before and after pictures clearly show the transformation. After an open day to celebrate their new grounds, one class shared some of their feelings about the project, from having fun at the planting day to enjoying the designing. The children planted bushes, and a rockery and storytelling area were introduced into the grounds. There is also a vegetable avenue that people can sit on the edge of.

Discussing the photographs
▶ Ask the children to describe the school grounds before and after the changes had been made. How do they think the children at the school feel now that their school grounds have been improved?
▶ Discuss what responsibilities and jobs they think the children will have, in order to keep the grounds in good condition.

IMPROVING THE ENVIRONMENT IN THE UK

▶ Ask the children to think about all the different materials that they can see and what they think the different areas are used for.

Activities

▶ As a class, mount a campaign to change something about your school environment. For example litter-picking, the way children travel to school, or looking after wildlife in the school grounds.

▶ Discuss if there is an area of the school that could be improved. Ask the children to devise a plan – providing a report and drawings – to show what could be done and how it could be maintained. Discuss and decide who would need to be involved if the plans went ahead. You could also contact the grounds maintenance department at the local council to come and advise the children on some of the issues to think about.

▶ Children will have different ideas about how the grounds should be changed so set up a role-play activity to explore issues around decision-making. Hold debates to argue the case for and against something.

▶ Ask the children to imagine and discuss what the school in the photographs will look like in 5, 10 or 15 years' time and then to do the same for your own school and its grounds.

Litter-picking, Planting

Improving the school environment doesn't have to mean drastic changes to the school grounds. Awareness can start with the simple act of litter-picking to increase the children's awareness of how much litter can accumulate around the school. Developing a garden or growing plants in a small area is also a good way to focus the children on improving the environment.

Public gardens

Whether you live in an inner-city area or a rural environment there are always public spaces for people to enjoy. While the responsibility for maintaining these public spaces is with the local council, everyone can play their part by being aware of environment and taking care of it – for example, by not dropping litter or pulling up the plants.

Discussing the photographs

▶ Look at the three images of the litter-picking, planting and the public gardens. Ask the children what the children and men in the photograph are doing? What is in the truck? Emphasise that all the people in the pictures are looking after their environment.

▶ Ask the children if there is a park or garden in their locality. Do they see their own local authority looking after the gardens? What do they think are the problems that the local authority has in keeping the environment clean and attractive?

▶ Talk about what is involved in litter-picking and the type of rubbish that the children would be likely to find in the school grounds and in other places.

▶ Discuss what the children think is involved in planting and looking after a tree, such as preparing the ground, feeding and watering the tree, protecting it from vandalism.

Activities

▶ Investigate whether litter is a problem in the school grounds. Are there any problem areas? Are there enough litter bins? Can the children suggest any solutions?

▶ Ask the children to using graphing software or spreadsheets to present evidence of the rubbish that has been found. The charts and graphs could form the basis of a display.

▶ Make up a 'care for the environment' trail around the school and its grounds.

▶ If the children become very keen to make some changes, they could take issues to the school council and look into arranging for the local authority and environmental organisations to come into school to assist them.

▶ All school grounds include areas that are valuable to wildlife. Conduct a wildlife survey to record the different birds, animals and insects that can be found.

▶ Discuss what type of habitats would encourage wildlife into the school grounds or into a park – for example, bird boxes and feeders, hedges and shrubberies for nesting sites, log and rock piles to provide habitats for insects.

▶ Conduct a tree survey and arrange a tree-planting day.

IMPROVING THE ENVIRONMENT IN THE UK

School council

A school council is an excellent way of involving the children in the way the school is run and including them in decisions that affect them. School councils are made up in a number of different ways. They normally have representatives from each class or year group, voted for by their peers. The school councillors are then responsible for making sure that they represent the views of the other children, as well as expressing their own opinion. This links very clearly to the United Nations Convention on the Rights of the Child which states in Article 12 that children have the right to express their opinion and for it to be taken seriously. School councils may have particular committees such as an environmental committee, or this may be a separate entity that feeds into the council. A school council would be especially pertinent when considering ways that children can improve their own environment.

Discussing the photographs
▶ Discuss the purpose of school councils or, if children are not familiar with them, explain what school councils are.
▶ Discuss the situation in your own school. Do the children think that having a school council is a good idea and why? If you do not have a school council, talk about the benefits of setting one up and what the challenges might be.
▶ Ask the children if they think their school environment could be improved by having an environmental club or committee, or do they think that it should be up to the school council to consider some of the issues raised in this chapter?

Activities
These activities can be run by a school council with the children working together to raise awareness throughout their school, not just in their own class.
▶ Plan to celebrate World Environment Day, which takes place in June each year. Put up posters in school and arrange special events and activities.
▶ Hold a class assembly on the subject of 'school and the environment'.
▶ Run a publicity campaign to raise awareness of environmental issues in school and in the wider community. Ask the children to produce posters and web pages and to design postcards to send to parents, encouraging them to be more environmentally friendly.
▶ Invite a guest to the school council to talk about an environmental issue that the children are concerned about. The council could then feed back to the rest of the school via class representatives, in an assembly or through a newsletter.

Videos: Noise in classroom, Noise outside classroom, Dinner hall

Noise affects people in school and is very much part of the school environment. It can cause problems for children as well as teachers, with variations in noise levels throughout the day. This video shows examples of such noise: before and when a class is settled; a dinner hall; and an example of noise outside school that can affect children's concentration. The difference between a noisy and quiet classroom is quite marked and it highlights just how difficult it can be for teachers to communicate when all the children are talking.

Discussing the videos
▶ Watch the videos together. Ask the children to watch and listen to how the noise levels change. Which of the clips is the noisiest and most disruptive to children in the school?
▶ Ask the children to listen to the noises from outside the school. Are there similar noises in the environment around their school? Do these noises affect them? Is there a way they can be reduced?

Activities
▶ As a class, make a list of the noise issues illustrated in the video clips.
▶ Discuss with the children how noise affects people in school and identify which noise causes the most problem – for example, the noise of children moving around the school.
▶ Divide the class into small groups. Ask them to tape the noise of children moving and undertake 'children counts' at set points around the school at different times of the day.
▶ Arrange for the groups to present their findings and to identify busy and quiet areas of the school at different times of the day.

NOTES ON THE PHOTOCOPIABLE PAGES

Word cards   PAGES 15–16

These cards contain some of the basic and more advanced vocabulary for the children to learn and use when looking at improving the environment in the UK. They include:
▶ words associated with citizenship
▶ words associated with environmental issues.

Read through the word cards with the children to familiarise them with the key words of the unit. Ask which words the children have heard before and clarify any they don't understand.

Activities
▶ Shuffle the cards and spread out a set of cards on each group's table. Ask the children to find specific words you call out.
▶ Use the cards as a word bank to help the children label pictures and to help them with longer pieces of writing.
▶ Begin a glossary with the words and include any other topic vocabulary used in the unit.

The environmental action tree   PAGE 17

This sheet shows a blank tree on which the children can write about some of the issues raised. It is a way of exploring possible actions they can take to improve the environment.

Activities
▶ As a class, write or make a symbol for the issue in question – for example, a bin could be drawn if the issue is recycling. This can be written or drawn onto the trunk.
▶ Devise symbols for possible actions and display these as fruit on the tree. Write the possible actions on the branches.
▶ Various resources and skills will be needed – for example, money, the local recycling officer, decision-making by the school council. Display these as the roots.
▶ Ask the children to look at the sheet individually and complete it for their own chosen issue. They should share their ideas in small groups and then share them with the rest of the class.
▶ Display the environmental action trees and discuss what the children have learned.

What we throw away   PAGE 18

This sheet is a way of recording the rubbish that the children have thrown away. It provides an opportunity to share knowledge and learn from each other. The children should record their own actions either at school or at home over a set period – for example, a school day, a weekend or a whole week.

Discussing the sheet
▶ Read through the sheet with the children as a class.
▶ Decide whether you will examine a collection of rubbish collected at school or whether the children will take this home and record evidence in their homes. The children could collect a bag of rubbish over a school day or week and fill in the sheet as a class or they could do this individually for themselves at home over a weekend.

Activities
▶ Ask the children to collect and record items of everyday rubbish to record on the sheet.
▶ Ask them to share their results in small groups and then share these as a whole class.
▶ Discuss the different types of rubbish collected and the materials they were made from.
▶ Make a display of some of the rubbish and the children's ideas about how the rubbish could be recycled or reused.
▶ Discuss how the children feel about the amount of rubbish we throw away and the consequences for the environment.
▶ Decide as a class and individually how to reduce the amount of rubbish thrown away.
▶ Ask the childen to find a good use for something they might throw away during the next week.
▶ Design a reduce, reuse and recycling charter for your classroom.

Citizenship word cards

IMPROVING THE ENVIRONMENT IN THE UK

| diversity |
| rights |
| needs |
| responsibility |
| global citizen |
| connections |
| poverty |
| respect |
| participation |

Enviromental issues word cards

IMPROVING THE ENVIRONMENT IN THE UK

| environment |
| sustainable |
| transport |
| global warming |
| pollution |
| journey |
| recycling |
| vehicles |
| planning |
| conserve |

The enviromental action tree

IMPROVING THE ENVIRONMENT IN THE UK

What we throw away

IMPROVING THE ENVIRONMENT IN THE UK

The collection began on _____ and lasted for _____

Item of rubbish	Was it necessary to throw away?	What materials it is made from?	How could it be reused or recycled?

GLOBAL CITIZENSHIP AND SUSTAINABLE DEVELOPMENT

Content and skills
This chapter links to Units 8, 16, 17, 18 and 24 of the QCA Scheme of Work for geography at Key Stage 2. The Global Citizenship and Sustainable Development Resource Gallery on the CD-ROM, together with the teachers' notes and photocopiable pages in this chapter, can be used when teaching these units.

As with the QCA units, this chapter encourages children to think about their own environment and the people who live there. It also reinforces and extends their knowledge and understanding of the wider world and encourages them to develop respect for human and natural diversity and take responsibility for their actions. The National Curriculum recognises that sustainable development is both one of the purposes of education and an explicit part of its values.

The teachers' notes contain background information about the resources and include ways of using them as a whole class, for group work or as individuals. Some of the activities link with other areas of the curriculum, such as RE, citizenship and PSHE. Wherever possible, the activities encourage the children to ask questions and develop an enquiring approach to their learning.

Resources on the CD-ROM
There is a photograph of children of different nationalities and of children looking at a globe. Different forms of transport such as trains, bicycles, cars and a metro tram are depicted. There are photographs of transport in Less Economically Developed Countries (LEDCs) including a rickshaw, car, wheelbarrow and motorbikes. Photographs of a school with photovoltaic panels are included to illustrate aspects of a sustainable school. There is an illustration of the Fairtrade Mark along with pictures of products and a series of photos to illustrate the journey of cocoa 'from bean to bar'. A map of Ghana and a Peter's Projection World map are also included.

Photocopiable pages
The photocopiable pages in the book are also provided in PDF format on the CD-ROM and can be printed from there. They include:
▶ word cards containing essential vocabulary for the unit
▶ 'The British', a poem by Benjamin Zephaniah
▶ a case study of a Ghanaian cocoa farmer's daughter
▶ the Development Compass Rose – a framework for understanding sustainable development
▶ a fair trade activity worksheet.

Geographical skills
Using the resources and activities in this chapter will develop the skills of photograph reading and interpretation, analysing and interpreting a range of secondary sources, identification of key features within visual images and the development of geographical vocabulary.

GLOBAL CITIZENSHIP AND SUSTAINABLE DEVELOPMENT

NOTES ON THE CD-ROM RESOURCES

WHAT IS GLOBAL CITIZENSHIP AND SUSTAINABLE DEVELOPMENT?

Oxfam defines a global citizen as someone who:
- is aware of the wider world and has a sense of their own role as a world citizen
- respects and values diversity
- has an understanding of how the world works economically, politically, socially, culturally, technologically and environmentally
- is outraged by social injustice
- participates in and contributes to the community at a range of levels from local to global
- is willing to act in order to make the world a more equitable and sustainable place
- takes responsibility for their actions.

The Panel for Education for Sustainable Development has outlined seven key concepts of sustainable development:

1. Interdependence. Understanding how people, the environment and the economy are inextricably linked at all levels from local to global.
2. Citizenship and stewardship. Recognising the importance of taking individual responsibility and action to ensure the world is a better place.
3. Needs and rights of future generations. Understanding our own basic needs and the implications for the needs of future generations of actions taken today.
4. Diversity. Respecting and valuing both human diversity (cultural, social and economic) and biodiversity.
5. Quality of life. Acknowledging that global equity and justice are essential elements of sustainability and that basic needs must be met universally.
6. Sustainable change. Understanding that resources are finite and that this has implications for people's lifestyles and for commerce and industry.
7. Balance. Understanding of uncertainty and of the need for precautions in action.

The Bruntland Report from the World Commission on Environment and Development (WCED) gave a definition of sustainable development: 'Sustainable development is development that meets the needs of the present without compromising the ability of future generations to meet their own needs. It contains two key concepts: the concept of needs, in particular the essential needs of the world's poor, to which overriding priority should be given; and the concept of limitations imposed by the state of technology and social organisation on the environment's ability to meet present and future needs.' (WCED, 1987)

GLOBAL CONNECTIONS

Multicultural group, Looking at the world

There are 193 countries in the world and in all of these countries children have the same basic needs and rights. These include the right to education, decent shelter, clean water, protection from abuse and neglect, the right to play and the right to express an opinion and be listened to. (See the UN Convention on the Rights of the Child available at www.unicef.org/crc/crc.htm for more information.) It is these kinds of things that connect children the world over.

It is important that children appreciate how countries are interdependent and that we all have global connections. Some of them will have relatives living in other countries, some will have visited or lived in other countries. Others will have seen a story on the television recently about a particular country. Even the clothes and shoes they wear will have been manufactured in a variety of countries.

In Britain there are 56 million people of at least 14 different faiths and speaking more than 300 languages. Multiculturalism should be presented to children as a positive thing and they should be aware and proud of their individuality – it would be boring if we were all the same!

Discussing the photographs

- Inform the children about the UN Convention on the Rights of the Child, to which 191 out of the world's 193 countries have signed up. Point out that even though the children in the 'Multicultural group' photograph look different, they all have the same basic needs and rights.

GLOBAL CITIZENSHIP AND SUSTAINABLE DEVELOPMENT

▶ Ask the children to think about what the children might be discussing in the 'Looking at the world' photograph. What have they used globes for?
▶ Ask the children which continent they can see on the globe. Explain that Africa is made up of 54 countries and that there will be differences as well as similarities between the countries so it is important not to generalise.
▶ Encourage the children to think about the different connections they have with the world. For example, how many countries have they visited? Do they have a friend or relative in another country?
▶ Ask the children what activities they have done so far today that required something from another country. They should think about the food they ate for breakfast, the programmes they watched on TV, where the car that they travelled to school in was made and so on.
▶ Talk about how we rely on other countries for certain things – for example, oil and foods such as cocoa, tea and bananas.
▶ What do the children think being a 'global citizen' means? Tell them Oxfam's definition. What are the advantages and disadvantages of being global citizens? As a class, devise your own definition of global citizenship.

Activities
▶ Ask the children to bring in objects that have global connections and find the places on a globe or map. (Check that your maps and globes are up to date.) Objects could be something that the child has brought back from holiday, a food from the kitchen cupboard or something that belongs to a relative.
▶ Make a list of the global connections that your locality has. For example, is it twinned with another town or village abroad? Is there a local industry that exports/imports products from abroad?
▶ Look at the Greenwich meridian line, which passes through the eight different countries of the UK, France, Spain, Algeria, Mali, Burkina Faso, Ghana and Togo. We all wake up at the same time and follow similar patterns to our days.
▶ Ask the children to find a newspaper or magazine story from or about another country.
▶ Put a collection of books about other countries and stories from other cultures in the book corner and borrow some artefacts from your schools library service or local development education centre.
▶ Make a 'Welcome' or 'Hello' poster for your classroom using languages from the countries that the children have connections with.
▶ Invite somebody into school from another country who now lives locally – ask them to tell the children the story of their journey to the UK and the similarities and differences between living in the UK and their country of origin.

Peter's Projection world map

Maps and atlases are important in developing children's images of the world. It is a good idea to introduce children to a range of maps as different types of maps exist for different purposes and we tend to have a restricted idea of how the world should look. The Peter's Projection map is known as an equal area map, as it shows the areas and proportions of countries more accurately than other maps. Countries of the south are portrayed more fairly as they are often portrayed as smaller than their actual size. There are, however, distortions on this map. The land masses appear elongated and land is stretched east to west near the poles and in a north to south direction near the Equator.

Discussing the map
▶ Remind the children of the number of continents and countries in the world.
▶ Ask the children to describe how the map looks different from maps they have seen before.
▶ Explain that the Peter's Projection Map shows countries in proportion to their relative sizes so more accurate comparisons between land areas are possible.
▶ Ask the children to locate the United Kingdom on the map. Is it how they expected it to look?

Activities
▶ Gather together different maps that you have in school and ask the children to bring in any world maps or atlases that they have at home. Look at the range of maps.

GLOBAL CITIZENSHIP AND SUSTAINABLE DEVELOPMENT

▶ Discuss which countries appear in the centre of maps and then, using a globe, explore how different countries can appear in the middle depending on your viewpoint. Point out how difficult it is to transfer the globe onto a flat piece of paper.
▶ Use the map to form a display with the children's names and global connections.

TRANSPORT

Every day, people across the world use different forms of transport to travel to places of work or to school, for leisure, to visit friends and to transport items. The form of transport used has an effect on the individual and on the environment both locally and globally. Children should understand the varying impacts and issues of the different forms of transport that they can use so that they can be involved in decision making. They also need to understand that where people live makes a difference to what types of transport they use.

Bicycle, Bicycle lane

More and more people are now choosing to travel to work and make other journeys by bicycle – and more cycle lanes, like the one shown in the photograph, are being built in our towns and cities. The National Cycle Network is a comprehensive network of safe and attractive routes to cycle throughout the UK. The network comprises nearly 16,000km of cycle routes. One third of these are on traffic-free paths; the rest follow quiet lanes or traffic-calmed roads. Visit the website www.nationalcyclenetwork.org.uk to find routes near your school. It is important to note, when looking at the photographs, that a safety helmet should always be worn when cycling, even on a cycle path.

Train

Trains are an alternative to cars and are a good form of public transport, particularly for long-distance journeys. Using railways has environmental advantages and having a good railway infrastructure is key to a sustainable transport system. Transport alone causes 25 per cent of the CO_2 emissions at a global level and road traffic and aviation are responsible for almost 90 per cent of this. A shift to using trains would help to reduce emissions.

Metro

Metros are often used in built-up areas where councils are trying to encourage public transport and reduce car use. The picture shows Manchester's 'Metrolink', the country's first modern street-operating light rail system. Since the Metrolink opened in 1992, many other towns and cities have opened light rail systems or are considering their viability. Other cities that have a similar transport systems are Sheffield, Nottingham and Newcastle. (London has the underground equivalent.) Metrolink runs through the city centre out to residential areas and is fast, frequent and convenient. The total network is approximately 37km in length and around 52,000 passenger journeys are made each day. Research suggests that at least 2 million car journeys have been taken off the road each year along the Metrolink corridor.

Rush hour in India, Rickshaw

Transport in LEDCs provokes all the same issues related to the environment and health as it does in this country. In the towns and cities of India, for example, there are many different modes of transport competing for space, ranging from cars and buses to bullock carts, people and rickshaws – both cycle and auto varieties! Traffic problems and pollution can be every bit as bad as in your local area. Rickshaws are a very common form of transport in India and other Asian countries. For further information on transport in India, see the notes and CD resources for 'Indian traffic' and 'Street in India' in the chapter 'Contrasting localities in India'.

Discussing the photographs

▶ Look at each photograph in turn and identify the forms of transport shown. Some photographs show more than one type.
▶ Ask the children what they think are the advantages and disadvantages of each form of transport. Discuss the alternatives that people could use.

GLOBAL CITIZENSHIP AND SUSTAINABLE DEVELOPMENT

▶ Which of these forms of transport have the children used and for what reasons? For example, if they used a train was it for a local or a long distance journey?
▶ What do the children think it would be like travelling in a rickshaw? What would it be like to be the driver of the rickshaw?
▶ Introduce the term 'sustainability'. Discuss children's ideas about how travel could become less damaging to the environment.

Activities
▶ Ask the children to find out about and discuss local transport issues.
▶ Investigate different forms of transport and routes around the local area including cars, buses, trams, trains, roads, footpaths and cycle lanes.
▶ Plan sustainable journeys around the local area to get to the school, shops and particular locations. How could it be easier or safer to walk or cycle to school?
▶ Conduct a survey of how children travel to school.
▶ Take the issue to the school council if you have one and write a policy to promote walking and cycling. Hold an assembly in school to share the children's findings.
▶ Discuss how goods have to be moved – use cocoa from Ghana as an example (see the notes later in this chapter).
▶ Using photographs or drawings of themselves using a form of transport, ask the children to consider questions such as: Where are you? Where are you going? What are you doing? What can you smell? How are you feeling?
▶ Make captions for the photographs on the CD for different purposes and audiences including an environmental organisation, a charity, a film advertisement, a tourist information centre. This will illustrate how easy it is to change the meaning of a photograph and how a situation can be interpreted in so many different ways.

ENVIRONMENTAL SUSTAINABILITY
Environmental sustainability is an issue for everyone around the world. The examples in this chapter illustrate this and show children how they are connected through these issues to people and countries across the globe. Living sustainably means not using up the Earth's resources at a faster rate than the Earth can generate them and not polluting the environment.

Kingsmead School, Photovoltaic panels

Kingsmead School has been designed on the principles of sustainable construction. Social, environmental, economic and environmental factors have all been considered. Local companies built the school and building materials were bought locally. Electricity is generated by a wind turbine and by photovoltaic panels. Rainwater is used to flush the toilets and the school monitors energy use as well as recycling and minimising waste. There is also a nature reserve in the school grounds. Inside the school there is a flexible teaching space. The children were involved in the design of the school and have written a green travel plan. The school meals are made using local produce. Low energy lighting with sensor controls and high insulation levels are further examples of how the school is sustainable. Further information about Kingsmead School can be found at www.kingsmead.cheshire.sch.uk.

There are many ways in which schools can become more sustainable – you do not have to build a new school! You could consider the following areas: energy, wildlife and biodiversity, transport, food, water, waste and resources, health and trade.

Discussing the photographs
▶ Tell the children that these pictures are of Kingsmead Primary School, the first school in the county of Cheshire to be built on the principles of environmental sustainability.
▶ Remind the children what sustainability is and ask them to give you some examples. Talk about why a sustainable school is good for the environment, both locally and globally. Do they think their school is an environmentally friendly school?
▶ Look at the pictures and discuss what the children think they show. Explain that the 'Photovoltaic panels' photograph shows a method of gathering solar energy and encouraging biodiversity.
▶ Have the children seen similar panels before? If so, where?

GLOBAL CITIZENSHIP AND SUSTAINABLE DEVELOPMENT

Activities
- Ask the children to list the sustainable features of their school and then to list what features they would include if they were architects designing a sustainable school.
- Invite the Local Agenda 21 officer into school. Their job is to promote initiative and action for sustainability in the local area.
- Develop and conduct a survey of staff, children and people at home about how the school could be improved in terms of sustainability.
- If the children become very keen to make some changes you could arrange for a local authority representative to come into school to listen to their concerns.

Solar panel in Morocco

This solar panel is in Morocco, North Africa. Morocco has a lot of sunshine so it makes sense to harvest sunlight. Homes and businesses that have solar panels supply their own power. Solar panels are also very useful in remote settlements that are not yet connected to the national grid, as well as providing a more environmentally friendly form of power. In some remote areas in Morocco, the only night-time light that people have comes from candles and paraffin lamps. People may also use small petrol generators or cables hooked up to truck batteries, to power televisions.

Discussing the photographs
- Remind the children what the climate is like in Morocco.
- Look at both of the images of solar panels and discuss the advantages for the school in the UK and for people in Morocco.
- Talk about why solar energy is environmentally friendly and what the energy generated could be used for.

Activities
- Design an energy efficiency programme for your school. For example: use natural light whenever possible, regulate classroom temperature, switch off computers when not in use.
- Discuss what the children consider to be typical energy requirements for their school and home. Do they believe this would be the same for people in Morocco or other LEDCs?
- Contact an organisation who can provide advice on energy efficiency. Look at the website www.think-energy.com

FAIR TRADE

The Fairtrade Mark, Fair trade products

Many farmers and workers in developing countries depend on selling basic goods such as tea, coffee and cocoa for their livelihoods. Yet prices fluctuate widely and often the producers do not get a fair share of the benefits of trade. Working conditions can be poor and wages are often low, with no job security. In 1993, the Fairtrade Mark was launched for products produced in developing countries and sold under fair trade regulations. The Fairtrade Foundation ensures basic rights for producers by offering fair and guaranteed prices and encouraging long-term trading commitments. The price they are paid always covers the cost of production no matter how low the market price goes. Fairtrade also upholds the principles of environmental sustainability, prohibits child labour and supports trade unions.

Since 1993, Fairtrade-certified products have increased to the extent that UK shoppers now buy over £100 million of Fairtrade-certified goods each year. A wide range of products is available from a growing number of supermarkets, newsagents, delicatessens and specific Fairtrade shops and more products are awarded the Mark each year. Looking at fair trade between countries gives children an opportunity to realise that they can actually change things, make informed choices and challenge unfairness.

Discussing the photographs
- Remind the children about what trade is and ask them to give you some examples.
- Ask the children if they have noticed the Fairtrade symbol anywhere. If so, where have they seen it?

GLOBAL CITIZENSHIP AND SUSTAINABLE DEVELOPMENT

▶ Consider the range of different products on the photograph and all the countries that these will have come from. Ask the children why we have to buy these products from abroad.
▶ Look at the Fairtrade Mark and discuss what they think it shows. Tell the children that it is awarded by the Fairtrade Foundation who regularly inspects suppliers to make sure that standards are being met. The symbol shows a cheering person. Ask the children if they can see this.
▶ Explain how fair trade helps producers in LEDCs.
▶ Ask the children to look for products showing the Fairtrade symbol the next time they go to the supermarket. Tea, coffee and bananas are easy to find.

Activities
▶ Ask the children to bring in a Fairtrade product or packaging and make a display. Use a map to illustrate where products come from. You could also make a collage of empty packaging.
▶ Hold a tasting session to compare the taste of fair trade and non-fair trade items.
▶ Discuss who benefits from fair trade but also discuss what the disadvantages are (and for whom).
▶ Plan to celebrate Fairtrade Fortnight, which happens nationally in March. Visit www.fairtrade.org.uk to find out the exact date and to see what events have been organised in the school's locality.
▶ If the children become very keen to support fair trade they could look into arranging for the school cafeteria or tuck shop to stock fair trade items or they could have a special stall.
▶ Run a publicity campaign to raise awareness of fair trade in school and in the wider community. Produce posters, web pages and design postcards to send to supermarkets and shops to encourage them to sell more fair trade products.

COCOA PRODUCTION IN GHANA

Map of Africa

'Dubble' is a fair trade chocolate bar which was launched by Comic Relief with the farmers' cooperative Kuapa Kokoo and the Day Chocolate Company. There are approximately two million cocoa farmers in Ghana and cocoa production is very important to the Ghanaian economy. Farmers mainly grow cocoa trees on small farms of two to three hectares. There is a government cocoa marketing board which is called Cocobod. Private companies buy the cocoa from the farmers and sell it on to Cocobod – which then sells it on to international buyers.

The image shows a map of Africa. Ghana is highlighted. The headquarters for the Kuapa Kokoo are located in Kumasi, but the farmers are spread throughout Ghana. Some farmers in Ghana are members of the Kuapa Kokoo cooperative, an association of cocoa farmers set up to develop fairer trading practices and to make sure that cocoa farmers get a good deal. They particularly benefit when their cocoa is sold to fair trade companies.

Cocoa pod on tree, Cutting pods down, Cutting pods open, Fermenting beans, Drying beans, Weighing beans, Processing chocolate in factory, Chocolate sold in shops

The journey from bean to bar is a long one. Cocoa trees grow in hot, damp climates in countries on or near the Equator. Ghana is one of these countries. The cocoa trees can grow up to five metres in height but they also need shade so other tall trees are planted around them. The trees take between three to five years to produce mature cocoa pods and each tree can produce more than 200 pods, like the ones shown in 'Cocoa pod on tree'. The pods grow on branches and also sprout from the trunk itself. They can be up to 35 centimetres long and are ready to be cut down when they turn yellow.

The pods have to be cut down from the tree using a special knife called a cutlass (see 'Cutting pods down'). The main harvest is October to February and there is a smaller one in June to July. The pods are placed in a big heap on the ground and they then have to be split open to get the gooey, sticky beans out (see 'Cutting pods open'). This has to be done

GLOBAL CITIZENSHIP AND SUSTAINABLE DEVELOPMENT

carefully to avoid damaging the beans. The beans are placed on banana leaves to dry out (see 'Fermenting beans') and left in a warm and shady place for five to seven days so that they can ferment. The banana leaf is folded over so that the beans are completely covered. It is the fermentation process that gives chocolate its special taste and colour. After the beans have fermented they need to be laid out in the sunshine to dry (see 'Drying beans'). This is normally done on bamboo drying racks which are made locally. It takes up to ten days for them to dry completely and be ready for the next stage of the journey. During this time they are regularly turned and any poor quality beans are taken out.

Once dry, the beans are placed in sacks and taken to be weighed (see 'Weighing beans'). The farmers can inspect the scales to make sure that they are set correctly and, because the cocoa is being sold to Kuapa Kokoo, the farmer will get a good price. The sacks of cocoa beans are transported to the Kuapa Kokoo warehouse at Kumasi and then taken by lorry to the port of Tema, where they are loaded onto a ship.

The cocoa then travels to Europe where it will be made into chocolate. Dubble bars are made at a factory in Germany. There are a number of processes that have to happen in order to change the cocoa into chocolate. The beans have to be roasted and then winnowed in order to get rid of their shells. They are then turned into cocoa butter and cocoa liquor and these are mixed together in a process called 'conching'. It is at this stage that milk, sugar, vegetable oil and any flavourings such as orange or vanilla will be added.

The photograph 'Processing chocolate in factory' shows the chocolate being tested for the correct consistency and flavour. It is only now that the chocolate can be formed into bars. The chocolate has to be transported again – this time to the UK where it is sold in shops and supermarkets. The photograph 'Chocolate sold in shops' shows Rijayatu, the daughter of a cocoa farmer (see photocopiable pages 33 and 34), holding two Dubble bars in a supermarket when she came to visit the UK. For more information visit the Dubble website at www.dubble.co.uk.

Discussing the photographs

▶ Ask the children if they know how chocolate is made. Tell them one of the key ingredients is cocoa and that these pictures show the process of production, from bean to bar.

▶ Look at the photographs and ask the children to suggest where they were taken and what the climate is like. Make sure they are aware of the location of Ghana in West Africa. Ask them why cocoa is not grown in the UK.

▶ Look at the photographs together and explain what is happening in each one.

▶ Consider the range of different foods that we eat that are imported. Why are raw products bought from abroad and then manufactured in Europe or the USA?

Activities

▶ Make a work chart to show what jobs are being done in each photograph and what evidence there is to support this.

▶ Ask the children to put the photographs in the correct order and to describe what is involved at each stage. They could also create a timeline for the cocoa growing year.

▶ Ask the children to write 'a day in the life' story of a cocoa farmer.

▶ In groups, challenge the children to come up with ideas or suggestions for using the pods once the beans have been scraped out. Explain that they are usually either turned into compost or they are burned and the ash is used to make a type of soap.

▶ Design a survey or questionnaire about the children's chocolate habits.

▶ Make a list of the problems that Ghanaian cocoa farmers face. Discuss how some of these problems might be solved by joining a fair trade cooperative.

▶ In groups, ask the children to mime the tasks shown in the photographs and then interview each other about what the job is like.

▶ Ask the children to find out what other ingredients apart from cocoa are needed to make chocolate. Where do these ingredients come from?

GLOBAL CITIZENSHIP AND SUSTAINABLE DEVELOPMENT

LOCAL MARKETS

UK farmers' market

Farmers' markets have stalls where the stallholders have grown, bred, brewed or baked the goods themselves. Their main emphasis is to help local producers and processors sell their goods direct to the public, near their source of origin. This has benefits for the producers, the environment and the local community. The selection of produce available at a farmers' market will vary with season and location. However, you are likely to be able to find a delicious selection of vegetables, fruit, meat, eggs, bread and cakes, jams and dairy produce.

Thai floating market

This is a picture of the famous Floating Market in Damnoen Saduak, 100km south of Bangkok in Thailand. At the market, you can watch the scene from the canal bank or take a boat to the market area. The sellers paddle up and down selling their produce along the canal sides. Unlike Westerners, Thais don't like to get suntanned, and will usually cover themselves up well. The market is agricultural, dealing mainly in fruits and vegetables. It opens early in the morning and closes at noon before the sun gets too hot and spoils the wares.

Floating markets are a connection with an older Thailand, when people lived on the banks of a canal and food vendors would travel from stilt house to stilt house in long-tailed boats, selling fresh produce. Nowadays, this bustling market is a draw for tourists who want to see a more unspoiled Thailand, far away from westernised Bangkok.

Discussing the photographs
▶ Remind the children that fair trade is also important for local farmers in the UK. These images show where local produce can be bought direct from the producer. They will not have been flown thousands of miles. Look at what is being sold in both markets. Can the children name the products? Would they be able to buy this type of produce elsewhere?
▶ Reinforce the concept of fair trade. Supporting local producers ensures that they receive a fairer return for their products, enabling them to invest in environmental and animal welfare improvements and maintain farm workers' employment. It also helps to sustain the local economy and cuts down on food transport miles.

Activities
▶ Discuss the advantages and disadvantages of eating just locally produced food.
▶ If there is a farmers' market in the locality, find out who goes there and what is sold.
▶ Locate Thailand and Damnoen Saduak on a map.
▶ Ask the children to write 'a day in the life' of a farmer at a UK farmers' market and at the Thai market – are there any similarities?

NOTES ON THE PHOTOCOPIABLE PAGES

Word cards   PAGE 30

In addition to the word cards provided on page 30, the word cards from the chapter 'Improving the environment in the UK' (pages 15 and 16) also support this unit. The word cards contain some of the basic and more advanced vocabulary for the children to learn and use when looking at global citizenship and sustainable development. They include words associated with:
▶ global citizenship and diversity
▶ transport and environmental issues
▶ cocoa production and fair trade.
Read through the word cards with the children to familiarise them with the key words of the unit. Ask which words the children have heard before and clarify any they don't understand.

Activities
▶ Shuffle the cards and spread out a set of cards on each group's table. Ask the children to find specific words you call out.

GLOBAL CITIZENSHIP AND SUSTAINABLE DEVELOPMENT

- Use the cards as a word bank to help the children label pictures and to help them with longer pieces of writing.
- Ask the children to describe the process of cocoa harvesting from bean to bar using the word bank.
- Begin a glossary with the words and include any other vocabulary used in the unit.

Global connections   PAGE 31

This sheet shows a child in the global web and some of the global connections they have. It also gives the children an opportunity to add more of their own ideas.

Discussing the sheet
- Read through the sheet as a class.
- Think about the global connections that the children have individually and as a school.

Activities
- Ask the children to look at the sheet and complete it for their own global connections.
- Ask them to share some ideas in small groups and then share these as a whole class.
- Discuss how many different countries are represented and remind them about what they've learned – about children's needs in all these countries and how similar these are.
- Ask the children to see how many of the countries they can find on maps and atlases.

'The British' poem   PAGE 32

This poem is a way of considering our global connections and examining the composition of Britain today. It provides an opportunity to consider the movement of people and the contribution that refugees have made to society. Some of the concepts and vocabulary are unfamiliar. Read it a couple of times and explain these before the children work individually.

Discussing the poem
- Tell the children that although the poem you are about to read is funny, it still contains a serious message. Read the poem at least once and ask the children what the message is.
- Ask the children if a member of their family originally came from another country.
- Ask them if they know someone who is one of the nationalities mentioned in the poem.
- What do they think the poet means by 'Add some unity, understanding and respect for the future'?

Activities
- Challenge the children to write a poem in the style of the original.
- Use a map to illustrate where all the countries mentioned in the poem are located.
- Ask the children to think about what would happen if the message of the poem is ignored. What can they do to make sure this does not happen?
- Ask them to find out more about diversity in the UK using the internet/reference books.

Rijayatu's story   PAGES 33–34

This sheet tells the story of a Ghanaian cocoa farmer's daughter. Rijayatu was 16 years old on 9 March 2004. She lives in a tiny village called Effiduase in Ghana with her two sisters Jamala and Adeshi and her mum and dad. Her parents are members of Kuapa Kokoo cocoa farmers cooperative. The cooperative was set up in 1993 and now has 40,000 members. In her story she tells of all the things she likes to do and what she hopes for the future. She explains how Fairtrade makes a real difference to her family. She visited the UK in 2003 during Fairtrade Fortnight and she is in the photograph 'Chocolate sold in shops'.

Discussing the text
- Read the text together then ask the children what they can tell you about Rijayatu. Was there anything about the story that surprised them?
- Discuss why Rijayatu can now go to school and why Fairtrade is so important to her family.
- Look at the cocoa farming photographs again and ask the children to imagine what Rijayatu thought when she visited the UK.

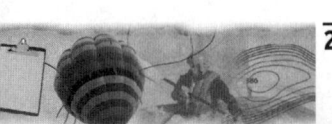

GLOBAL CITIZENSHIP AND SUSTAINABLE DEVELOPMENT

Activities
- Ask the children to write about a day in the life of Rijayatu.
- Working in groups, ask the children to discuss the similarities and differences between Rijayatu's life in Ghana and their lives in the UK.
- Get the children to write a letter to Rijayatu asking her about her life in Ghana.

The development compass rose — PAGE 35

The development compass rose is an excellent framework for encouraging children to ask questions about any place or situation. It can be placed on any photograph, locality or artefact to help ask a range of questions about four aspects of development. These are: natural/ecological questions, economic questions, social and cultural questions and 'who decides'/political questions. It provides a way of looking at issues locally, nationally and globally and the links that exist between them.

Activities
- Look at any of the photographs provided and place it in the middle of the whiteboard. Refer to the development compass rose and, as a class, generate questions about the photograph that relate to each point of the compass.
- In small groups, ask the children to choose a photograph. They should place it in the centre of a large sheet of paper and generate questions using the development compass rose. For the diagonal points of the compass, they should consider questions that raise, for example, both economic and social issues.
- Share the children's ideas and compare whether similar questions or issues have arisen.
- Make a giant compass rose using the questions generated in the previous activity. Working in small groups, ask the children to rephrase their questions into key questions that could be applied to any of the images on the CD and to write them on a strip of paper. On a large sheet of paper, write the four issues at the points of the compass and ask groups to add their questions at appropriate points.
- Discuss the questions and, as a class, decide if they are all in the correct place.
- Look at all the photographs in this chapter and consider whether any of the questions could be applied to all the images.

Fair trade role cards — PAGE 36

The role cards are intended to make children think about the reality of how much the cocoa farmers get from the sale of their cocoa. They also provide an opportunity to consider all the different people, jobs and costs in the chocolate-making process. It is often not the growers who gain most from the sale of products such as chocolate. There are others in the chain from bean to bar who benefit significantly more. Children should be made aware that the information in this unit can be applied to other food products.

Activities
- Divide the class into groups of four children. The children will take on the role of different people involved in the production, sale and purchase of chocolate. These are the cocoa farmers, a luxury chocolate company, shopkeepers and consumers.
- Ask the children to look at their role cards. The farmers, shopkeepers and managers of the chocolate company should consider what is involved in their job. Do they have large costs to cover? How much money do they think they should receive?
- Look at the CD images to see just how much work is involved for the different groups.
- Ask each group to develop a role-play in which the cocoa farmer, chocolate company and shopkeeper have a discussion with the consumer about how much money they should receive from the sale of a bar of chocolate costing £1.
- Gather the groups' ideas on how much money they think they should get out of the £1.
- Reveal to the children how the £1 from the proceeds of the sale is broken down: the chocolate processing and manufacturing companies get 40.5p, the shopkeepers 28p, the UK Government 17.5p in VAT, the Ghanaian Government 7p, the Ghanaian cocoa growers 7p.
- Discuss the children's reactions to these figures. Do they think this is fair? Can they think of ways that the cocoa farmers could benefit more?
- Discuss fair trade as an alternative and design a campaign to promote it.

Cocoa production word cards

cocoa

cooperative

fair trade

Ghana

products

farmer

sustainability

Global connections

GLOBAL CITIZENSHIP AND SUSTAINABLE DEVELOPMENT

- MUSIC/ENTERTAINMENT
- RELATIVES/FRIENDS/NEIGHBOURS
- TRAVEL/HOLIDAYS
- SCHOOL SUBJECTS
- TV PROGRAMMES
- CLOTHES
- HOBBIES
- FOOD

'The British' poem

THE BRITISH
Serves 60 million

Take some Picts, Celts and Silures
And let them settle
Then overrun with the Roman conquerors.

Remove the Romans after approximately four hundred years
Add lots of Norman French to some
Angles, Saxons, Jutes and Vikings, then stir vigorously.

Mix some hot Chileans, cool Jamaicans, Dominicans,
Trinidadians and Bajans with some Ethiopians,
Chinese, Vietnamese and Sudanese.

Then take a blend of Somalians, Sri Lankans, Nigerians
And Pakistanis,
Combine with some Guyanese
And turn up the heat.

Sprinkle some fresh Indians, Malaysians, Bosnians,
Iraqis and Bangladeshis together with some
Afghans, Spanish, Turkish, Kurdish, Japanese
And Palestinians
Then add to the melting pot.

Leave the ingredients to simmer.

As they mix and blend allow their languages to flourish
Binding them together with English.

Allow time to be cool.

Add some unity, understanding and respect for the future
Serve with justice
And enjoy.

Note: All the ingredients are equally important. Treating one ingredient better than another will leave a bitter, unpleasant taste.

Warning: An unequal spread of justice will damage the people and cause pain ...

Give justice and equality to all.

by Benjamin Zephaniah

Rijayatu's story

GLOBAL CITIZENSHIP AND SUSTAINABLE DEVELOPMENT

Rijayatu was 16 years old on 9 March 2004. She lives in a tiny village called Effiduase in Ghana. In the village, there is one main road, a well, a church, lots of wattle-and-daub houses, a road ambling down to a valley in the forest and cocoa farms. The village is surrounded by lush green vegetation including cocoa, casava, plantain and banana trees.

Rijayatu lives with an extended family – a big, big family. As well as her mum and dad and two sisters Jamala and Adeshi, her grandmother, uncle, aunt and cousins all live with them. They eat together, dance together – do everything together. Their house has eight rooms. It's made of bricks but has not been painted. Rijayatu shares a room with her two sisters, granny and her mum.

Rijayatu's parents are cocoa farmers. Her grandfather was also a cocoa farmer. Rijayatu helps on the farm by gathering sticks for the firewood when she has finished her school work. She has tried to help her father ever since she was young. When it is the harvest she helps gather up the pods and fetches fresh water for the seedlings. The water is quite a distance from the farm so she has to carry the water in buckets. The farm is more than five acres so lots of water is needed. After helping on the farm in the evenings, Rijayatu goes home and cooks. She sometimes cooks her favourite food which is fufu (a kind of dumpling) with groundnut soup and chicken. She likes that very much.

Rijayatu doesn't like the cocoa season. They have to wake up very early – around 5am, the time of the cockerel – to do the planting. It is best to plant seedlings before the sun rises otherwise the soil becomes very hard.

Image and text (based on an interview in 2002) © The Day Chocolate Company

GLOBAL CITIZENSHIP AND
SUSTAINABLE DEVELOPMENT

Rijayatu's story

Rijayatu's parents are members of Kuapa Kokoo cocoa farmers' cooperative. The cooperative was set up in 1993 and now has 40,000 members. Kuapa Kokoo owns a third of The Day Chocolate Company, who produce the fair trade 'Divine' and 'Dubble' chocolate bars for UK supermarkets and stores.

Rijayatu knows all about fair trade. One day she asked her father how he became a cocoa farmer. He didn't want to tell her – he said she was a kid and too young to ask about this, so she went and cooked with her mother who told her more.

Before her father joined the Fairtrade organisation, he did not get a fair price for the cocoa he produced. When he joined Fairtrade he got a much better price. He also gets a bonus at the end of the year for each bag of cocoa that sells. Rijayatu likes Fairtrade and it makes her feel very happy.

Rijayatu has met children in the UK through the Fairtrade bar 'Dubble'. She has been involved in a project called Dubble Lives. They get to know people in the UK through computers. They learn how to use computers and the internet and can connect to people all over the world. Rijayatu also had a chance to eat her first sweet chocolate, Dubble, which she thinks is delicious.

In the future Rijayatu would like to be a scientist and find a cure for AIDS. She needs three years of secondary school and four years of university to do this. Rijayatu was worried that her family might not be able to afford for her to go to university, so she is helping her parents on the farm as much as she can. Since her parents joined Fairtrade, however, things are improving and Rijayatu's worries are flying away.

The development compass rose

GLOBAL CITIZENSHIP AND SUSTAINABLE DEVELOPMENT

A framework for understanding sustainable development

Natural
These are questions about the environment – energy, air, water, soil, living things and their relationship to each other. These questions are about the 'built' as well as the natural environment.

Who decides?
These are questions about power – who makes choices and decides what is to happen, who benefits and loses as a result of these decisions, and at what cost.

Economic
These are questions about money, trading, aid, ownership, buying and selling.

Social
These are questions about people, their relationships, their traditions, culture and the way they live. They include questions about how, for example, gender, race, disability, class and age affect social relationships.

From the Development Compass Rose/TIDE Consultation Pack © 1995, DEC (Birmingham) Tide Centre, Birmingham

Fair trade role cards

Cocoa farmer

You have been growing cocoa for many years. It is your family's only source of income. You have a small piece of land on which you grow cocoa. It is a hard job as there is always a lot to do to look after the trees. Harvests happen in October to February and in June and July. The money that you earn is needed to pay for things for the house, health care and for your children to go to school. Last year things were difficult because some of the trees got Black Pod disease and less cocoa was harvested.

Luxury chocolate company

You are the manager of a luxury chocolate company and you buy the cocoa from Ghana. It is then brought to your factory in Germany where ingredients such as sugar, milk and flavourings are added. These all have to be bought by your company. You believe that in the whole bean-to-bar process, this is the most important stage. You have wages and other costs to cover such as machinery and packaging for the chocolate you produce. In order to sell the chocolate you have to advertise and promote your product widely. This is expensive and there is a lot of competition from other companies.

Shopkeeper

You have a small shop which a lot of local people visit and you get many children coming into the shop after school. You buy the chocolate and keep it until you can sell it. There are several things that you have to spend money on. The rent of the shop is quite high, for example, as it is in a busy place. You also have to keep the shop looking attractive so that customers will come in and you are open for long hours so have quite a lot of staff salaries to pay. Selling chocolate and sweets does not make you much money because these items are not very expensive for people to buy so you have to sell a lot of them. You also have a house and family to buy things for.

Consumer

You are a big fan of chocolate and buy at least one bar every week. You do not always buy the same bar as you like to try different varieties. You buy chocolate using your pocket money and you never really think about the price as you enjoy eating it so much. Nor have you thought about how the chocolate gets to the shop and what is actually in the bars. You didn't know that farmers in Ghana were involved in the process!

SETTLEMENTS

Content and skills
The content of this chapter supports the activities in Unit 9 of the QCA Scheme of Work for geography, 'Village settlers' – a unit with a distinctive focus on historical geography and close links to units in the Scheme of Work for history. It supports the unit by providing some necessary resources for exploring ideas related to settlement origins, sites and development. The content updates, augments and extends the unit by looking at a range of different settlements and by exploring the concept of settlement hierarchies at an appropriate primary level. Use of the content will aid the development of children's visual literacy skills and, specifically, their ability to gather information from maps.

Resources on the CD-ROM
The resources include images of a specific village and other settlements in a defined geographical area – the English Lake District. There are images conveying the characteristics of other settlement types – city and conurbation – and factors in settlement location, such as protection. The hierarchy of settlements in a locality is illustrated through a video sequence. Maps are provided to indicate the features of a typical historical settlement and to support the investigation of place names in a locality as clues to early settlement.

Photocopiable pages
The photocopiable resources within the book will enable children to organise and communicate their findings about settlement hierarchies and origins. They are also provided in PDF format on the CD and can be printed from there. They include:
▶ word cards
▶ a diagram of a settlement hierarchy
▶ a worksheet on place name origins.

Geographical skills
Using the resources and activities in this chapter will develop the skills of map reading and interpretation, identification of key features within visual images and the development of geographical vocabulary.

Image © Tony Pickford

SETTLEMENTS

NOTES ON THE CD-ROM RESOURCES

UK map

This map shows the location of the English Lake District in relation to the rest of the UK. The Lake District is an area of mountains, hills and lakes in the county of Cumbria in the north-west of England. Although relatively small in size (the National Park area is 2292km^2), the Lake District is the site of England's highest mountain Scafell Pike (978m) and its deepest lake, Lake Windermere. The area shows strong evidence of Viking settlement through place names such as Satterthwaite, Keswick and local terms used to describe physical features – tarns (small lakes), becks (streams) and fells (hills). Settlement by other groups can also be discerned – the name of the mountain Helvellyn is a Celtic word meaning 'yellow moor' and Coniston, at the heart of the district, is a Saxon-influenced place name meaning 'the king's manor'.

Settlement patterns in the Lake District are dominated by the landscape – villages and small towns have developed in the valleys between the fells as service centres for local agriculture and, more recently, as centres for tourism. The fells themselves are close-cropped by hill sheep and, although the landscape gives an impression of timeless continuity, human impact has been great – the fells are criss-crossed, even at the highest levels, by drystone walls and, in the most popular walking areas, footpath erosion is a serious problem. Further information about the district can be found in *About the National Park*, a publication for Key Stage 2 produced by the National Park Authority. A PDF of the publication can be found at www.lake-district.gov.uk.

Discussing the map

▶ Ask the children to describe the location of the Lake District. For example, is it in the south-west, the north-west or the north-east of England?
▶ Discuss the location of the Lake District in relation to the school's locality. What direction is the Lake District? How long do you think it would take to get there by car, bus or train?
▶ What do the children think the landscape is like in the Lake District?
▶ What types of settlement would the children expect to find in the area – cities and large towns or smaller towns and villages? Why?

Activities

▶ Print out the map of the UK and ask the children to mark the school locality on it. Working in groups, ask them to use road atlases to plan routes to the Lake District from the school locality. Record the routes on blank outline maps of the UK – suitable maps can be found at www.ordnancesurvey.co.uk/oswebsite/freefun/outlinemaps.
▶ Ask the children to record their predictions about the landscape and the settlements of the Lake District on a chart. They could then compare their predictions to photographs from the district as a whole.

Animation: Settlement hierarchy

This animation shows an example of a settlement hierarchy in a locality and is a good visual introduction to the study of settlements. A helicopter flies over a sequence of settlements from a farm to a village to a town. The settlements are shown in plan view with a river linking them. The helicopter's shadow can be seen on the ground – point this out to the children, as they may be puzzled by this moving shape. The settlement types shown are:
▶ farms – usually single dwellings, with outbuildings, occupied by one family;
▶ a village – a small settlement, usually with a church and limited services, such as a post office, telephone box and public house;
▶ a town – a larger settlement, with all the services offered by a village, plus additional features such as a bus and/or railway station, a town hall and a hospital.

Discussing the animation

▶ Show the initial screen and ask the children what it shows. As necessary, explain that the view shows a helicopter from above flying over some settlements.
▶ Ask the children to identify the settlements that the helicopter flies over. Ask them to note

SETTLEMENTS

the settlement labels and the appearance of the settlements from above. Run the animation from start to finish.
▶ Ask the children about the characteristics of the three settlement types. Run the animation again, focusing the children's attention on the differing sizes of the settlements and on the features in each one. Ask them to count the number of buildings in the village and compare it to the town.
▶ Ask the children about any settlement types that are missing from the animation (hamlets, which are bigger than farms but smaller than villages). Also ask about the next settlement up in the hierarchy.

Activities
▶ Get the children to make a series of captioned and annotated pictures to show either a complete settlement hierarchy, including hamlets, and concluding with a city or a sequence of settlements in the school's locality.
▶ Ask the children to write a brief pilot's log describing what can be seen from the helicopter.

OS map of the Lake District

This map shows an area of the central Lake District in Cumbria with a range of different settlement types in evidence. This resource is most useful as a means of demonstrating how a map can enable us to identify different types of settlements in a locality. The settlement types shown include hamlets (for example, Outgate and Clappersgate), villages (for example, Hawkshead and Crosthwaite) and towns (for example, Windermere). The map illustrates clearly that the smaller the size of settlement the more of that type of settlement there are in a locality. The impact of physical features on settlement patterns is also illustrated by the map – the settlements are all situated in valleys between the hills and the size and development of many has been restricted by the landscape.

Discussing the map
▶ Explain which area is shown in this map. Ask the children what the map suggests about the landscape in this part of the UK. How does it show landscape features?
▶ Discuss the sizes of the different settlements shown on the map. Can the children see any very small settlements? How are these shown on the map? What is the largest settlement on the map? Is this a town or a city? How do they know?
▶ Explain to the children the difference between a hamlet and a village. Point to any of the hamlets and ask the children to identify which type of settlement this is. Now point to a village and ask them what type of settlement this is. How do they know it is a village? Finally, point out the differences in size (the grey shading) and numbers of symbols showing facilities. Which are the most common types of settlement on the map? Which are the least common?
▶ Point out a hamlet on the map. Ask the children to guess where people who live there might go to shop for everyday items such as newspapers or bread. Ask them if there is anywhere on the map where they think people might go to shop for clothes or to buy a new washing machine.

Activities
▶ Ask the children to make a chart listing examples from the map of different settlement types – hamlet, village, small town, larger town.
▶ Ask the children to identify which settlement types on the settlement hierarchy diagram (see photocopiables section) are not on the map (large town upwards). Ask them to count or estimate the number of each of the different settlement types on the map.

Farm

This isolated farm is in a valley near Coniston in the Lake District. Farms are the lowest form of settlement in a hierarchy of settlements. Within the hierarchy, higher-order settlements, such as cities and towns, are relatively few in number and lower-order settlements, such as villages, hamlets and farms, are common. Although the concept is an entirely artificial categorisation devised by geographers to explain the distribution of settlements, it has value at primary level to help children explain the pattern of settlements on a map and the links between settlements of different sizes. As a settlement, the farm has an agricultural function and provides shelter and employment for its residents. In an area such as the Lake District a farm may also offer accommodation to tourists.

Discussing the photograph
▶ Talk about and list the human and physical features in the picture. Note that the drystone walls are a man-made feature.
▶ Explain that the farm in the picture is an example of the most basic form of settlement. Ask the children to list the functions of a farm – for example, growing crops or rearing animals, shelter, employment, possibly providing accommodation for visitors.
▶ Ask the children to predict what animals might be reared on this farm. Why?

Activities
▶ With the children working in small groups, ask them to make a chart listing the advantages and disadvantages of this settlement site. Ask them to explain why they think the farm has not grown into a larger settlement.
▶ Challenge the children to write a short newspaper advertisement for the farm as a holiday bed and breakfast destination. Make sure the text appeals to the tourists who might want to stay on the farm, for example ramblers rather than those looking for entertainment and nightlife.

Hamlet

This photograph shows a hamlet – the next settlement up in the hierarchy of settlements after a farm. Unlike an isolated farm, it is a place with several buildings grouped loosely together and it may be home to five or six families. A hamlet can be distinguished from a village by its small size and by its lack of services and amenities. In a rural locality, there are likely to be many hamlets – providing homes for agricultural workers and, nowadays, homes for people who commute to work in nearby larger settlements. In tourist areas, such as the Lake District or the Scottish Borders, houses in quiet hamlets are often bought as second homes by town and city dwellers.

The picture shows several features that are characteristic of rural hamlets and give clues as to why the settlement has not developed into a village or town. The setting is rural and the road infrastructure seems limited, the land is undulating and the site appears to be rather exposed.

Discussing the photograph
▶ Talk about the physical and human features in the photograph.
▶ How many buildings can the children see? What type of buildings do they appear to be? (homes, with some outbuildings). What materials do they think have been used to construct the buildings? Why do they think these materials have been used?
▶ Talk about the clues in the picture that tell you that this settlement is in the countryside, – for example, fields and scattered buildings.
▶ Explain that the picture shows most of the whole settlement, not just part of a village. Explain that the settlement is not a village because of its small size and lack of services. What services can you see in the picture? The lack of a place of worship is one way in which a hamlet can be distinguished from a village.

Activities
▶ Ask the children to look at the photograph of a farm (provided on the CD) and identify the differences between the hamlet and the farm.
▶ Make a sketch of the picture and annotate it – this will encourage close observation of physical and human features. Label features, such as the houses and the materials used to build them, the stone walls, the woodland, and so on.
▶ Ask the children to record the characteristics of a hamlet to distinguish it from a farm and a village – for example, it is home to several families, but lacks services.
▶ Either on paper or using a computer-based map-making program, the children can create a map of a fictional rural locality showing the distribution of farms and hamlets – there should be many farms with a smaller number of hamlets in between them.

SETTLEMENTS

Hawkshead village: view 1, view 2, view 3

The photographs show views of Hawkshead, a village in the central Lake District. Like many villages in this area, it is mainly built from local, whitewashed stone and, although it was originally settled for other reasons, it now has an economy which is greatly dependent on tourism. In the hierarchy of settlements, a village like this one lies between a hamlet and a small town. A village can be quite small but it usually has more services and functions than a hamlet – there may be a local shop, post office, primary school and a public house. One distinguishing feature will be the presence of a place of worship, usually a church. Small shops, a pub and a church can be seen in the photographs.

In contrast to a small town, a village is unlikely to have a wide range of shops or a large supermarket. Residents will usually have to travel to the nearest town for medical services and children will have to travel to a secondary school in a town nearby or to a school that serves the needs of several villages.

A village usually has a population of no more than a few hundred people. In the Lake District, however, village populations can fluctuate greatly. In the summer season, hotels and inns play host to visitors and many villages have some houses used as second homes by town and city dwellers. Such homes will only be occupied during holidays and at weekends, lying empty on weekdays for most of the year.

Discussing the photographs

▶ Ask the children what type of settlement they think the pictures show. Ask them if they think it is a large or small settlement.
▶ Ask the children how they think the settlement differs from a hamlet. What features and/or services can they see that were not in the hamlet?
▶ Discuss and list the human and physical features that can be seen in the pictures (buildings, roads, landscape, and so on).
▶ Explain to the children that the image shows a village and one distinguishing feature of a village is the presence of a place of worship, usually a church. Ask them about places of worship that they know in their locality. How do they think these places of worship might compare to a village church?

Activities

▶ Ask the children to make a chart comparing the village and its features to (a) the hamlet previously studied and (b) to their own locality. They should use headings such as buildings, roads, shops, services, physical features.
▶ The issue of second homes is highly contentious in areas, such as the Lake District. Split the children into groups and ask them to take on the role of either a local resident or second home buyer. What points would each make about the issue?

Small town

A town is a middle-order settlement in the hierarchy of settlements. Many towns, like this one, have grown and expanded from village settlements. Reasons for expansion are varied. In the case of the small town in the picture, Bowness-on-Windermere in Cumbria, the growth was spurred by the opening of a railway station at nearby Birthwaite in 1847. Until then, Bowness had been a relatively isolated village on the shore of Lake Windermere, visited only by a few wealthy travellers. With the coming of the railway, many more visitors came from the industrial towns of northern England for day trips and longer stays, prompting the growth of shops and services, such as inns and hotels. The result can be seen in the picture – the village expanded up the hillside away from the lake. The relatively narrow streets built at that time could accommodate the horse-drawn transport of the 19th century but are now inadequate for the heavy traffic that comes into the town during the summer tourist season.

Bowness is a representative small-town settlement in that it has a population of about 8500 (boosted by large numbers of visitors in the summer) and it has a range of shops and services, not normally found in a village. There are some specialist shops (mainly catering for tourists), small supermarkets, banks, doctors and dentists. There are regular bus services serving the town and a large secondary school on the outskirts, which draws children from neighbouring villages, hamlets and farms. However, Bowness lacks some of the facilities found in larger towns; there is no bus station, hospital, leisure centre or weekly market. Its growth is limited by the hilly landscape, problems of waste water disposal and its location in a National Park area.

Discussing the photograph
▶ Ask the children what clues in the picture tell them that this is a small town, not a village. Are there any clues that tell them that this is a place that attracts visitors?
▶ Ask the children to compare the place in the picture to their own locality. How is it similar/different?
▶ Are there any clues that tell you that the street in the foreground of the picture is older than the main street in the background? (cobbles)

Activities
▶ Ask the children to record the characteristics of a small town to distinguish it from a village and from a larger market town, for example it has many more services than a village, but lacks some key facilities, notably a weekly market.
▶ Ask the children to make a chart comparing Bowness to their school locality. They should use headings such as 'roads and traffic', 'building materials', 'visitors' and 'landscape'.
▶ Explain that Bowness has grown because it is a popular tourist destination. Nowadays traffic is a major problem in the town because few visitors use the nearby railway, instead preferring to come by car or coach. Ask the children to design a poster encouraging people to visit the town by rail.

Market town

Market towns are middle-order settlements in the settlement hierarchy. They offer more shops, services and facilities than villages, but do not tend to have the large-scale retail facilities or the specialist shops found in higher-order settlements. Most market towns in the UK will have developed as service and trading centres for agricultural communities and are likely to be characterised by the holding of an outdoor and/or an indoor market on one or more days of the week. Usually market towns are situated at the crossroads of several routes and have good transport links. They may be at the site of important bridges over rivers.

This photograph shows an outdoor market in the market square of Keswick in the north of the Lake District. It is a busy, bustling scene with shoppers gathered around the stalls and on their way to other shops and services in the square. The moot hall dominates the square and, in the background, the surrounding fells can be seen. The moot hall dates from 1571 when it was built as a court house. Since then it has been used as a market hall, prison and town hall.

Discussing the photograph
▶ Ask the children to list the features they can see in the picture and to give the picture a title.
▶ Sort the features into permanent and temporary features of the market square.
▶ Sort the features into familiar and unfamiliar ones, in comparison to the school locality.
▶ Ask the children to compare the market stalls to other shops that will be in the market square – how are the market stalls different from other shops? Why do they think the stallholders might be able to sell goods more cheaply?
▶ Ask the children what they think the shopkeepers in the square think about the market.

SETTLEMENTS

Do they think the market is good or bad for the other shopkeepers? (Shopkeepers would possibly dislike the extra competition that the market brings but would value the increased numbers of people and trade.)
▶ Ask the children to look for clues in the picture that tell them the size of this settlement. How can we tell that that this place is bigger than a village, but smaller than a city? (For example, the size and height of buildings around the square suggests a large settlement, but the proximity of the hills suggests that the settlement is smaller than a city.)

Activities
▶ If there is a market in their own locality, ask the children to make a chart recording similarities and differences between this market and the market that they know.
▶ Using a 1:50,000 scale OS map, ask the children to identify and list market towns in the vicinity. Provide children with criteria to help to identify market towns (detailed above).
▶ Encourage the children to use reference materials to research the origins of fruit that come from overseas (for example, oranges, grapefruit and lemons). Make a display featuring an image of a market stall selling fruit and vegetables with arrows to a world map. The display should emphasise interdependence and the range of places that may supply produce to a local market.

City centre street

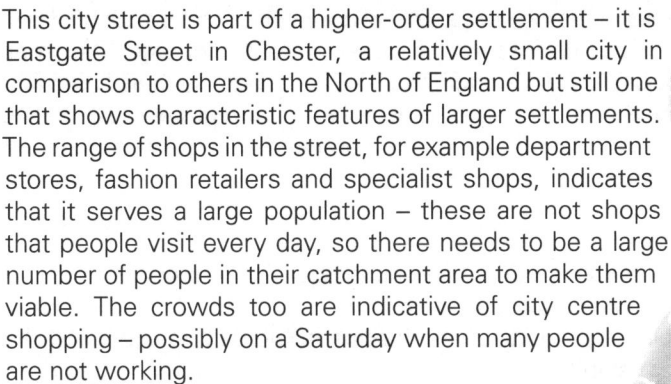

This city street is part of a higher-order settlement – it is Eastgate Street in Chester, a relatively small city in comparison to others in the North of England but still one that shows characteristic features of larger settlements. The range of shops in the street, for example department stores, fashion retailers and specialist shops, indicates that it serves a large population – these are not shops that people visit every day, so there needs to be a large number of people in their catchment area to make them viable. The crowds too are indicative of city centre shopping – possibly on a Saturday when many people are not working.

The public transport that is evident also indicates a higher-order settlement. Although buses and taxis may be found in places further down the settlement hierarchy, it is only in cities that they are found in large numbers alongside more innovative and uncommon transport systems, such as trams and underground railways. Transport has become a key issue of city centre living. People are being encouraged to use public transport, as opposed to private cars, to visit city centres because streets soon get jammed and many city centres have insufficient parking spaces.

Discussing the photograph
▶ Ask the children to identify the different types of shops they can see in the picture. Emphasise that they should suggest 'types' and not just names of shops.
▶ Ask the children to identify other clues in the picture that tell them that this is a large settlement or city. (Crowds, lots of buses, other traffic in the distance.)
▶ Ask the children to identify the different forms of transport they can see in the picture. How many of these can be found in the school locality?
▶ How often do the children visit a large shopping centre like this one? Every day, every week or less often?
▶ The white bus in the foreground of the picture is an example of one way in which city authorities are trying to reduce car traffic. What does 'Park & Ride' usually mean?

Activities
▶ Ask the children to make a chart identifying similarities and differences between the shopping centre in the picture and a local shopping centre.

▶ Set up a role-play scenario in which the local council in a city wants to bring in a congestion-charging scheme that will encourage people to use public transport rather than cars. What would different people and interest groups in the city centre think about this? Put the children into small groups and prepare a case for a 'public meeting'. Roles could include: the owner of a large store, someone who works in a city centre shop, a taxi driver, the owner of a bus company, a shopper who usually travels to the centre by car, a traffic warden, a resident of the city centre, and so on. In such a scenario, views would be polarised between those who welcome the quieter streets and reduced pollution, and those who fear that the congestion charge would discourage shoppers and harm trade.

Manchester – urban renewal

As well as providing extensive shopping facilities, cities at the centre of conurbations, such as Manchester, also have functions not found in other settlements. They are, for example, religious and cultural centres usually with large cathedral churches and museums and galleries holding nationally important collections. In the picture you can see Manchester Cathedral and, in the background, the relatively new Urbis Museum. The latter, in its high-tech, glass-fronted building, is a museum of city life, contrasting past and modern-day life in Manchester with lifestyles in other world cities.

This part of Manchester, known as the Millennium Quarter, is an example of a city area that has undergone redevelopment and renewal. Like other UK cities, Manchester has experienced a period of decline, as old industries have closed down and many residents have moved out of the city centre area. With the growth of more modern 'industries', such as financial services, city centres have been redeveloped and new buildings, such as Urbis and the nearby 'Printworks' leisure centre, are symbols of renewal attracting people back to live in the city centre. Other cities in the north of England, such as Leeds and Newcastle-upon-Tyne, have undergone similar processes of renewal.

Discussing the photograph
▶ Tell the children where the picture was taken and discuss how the two buildings in the picture are different. Which one is newer? How do they know?
▶ Most cities have large cathedral churches, such as the one in the picture. How is it the same/different to a local place of worship?
▶ Which of the two buildings do the children prefer? Why? Which building would they like to visit?
▶ Explain that Urbis is an important, modern museum built to celebrate the Millennium in the year 2000. Have the children seen, heard of or visited any other buildings or features that were built at this time?
▶ List words that can be used to describe (a) the Cathedral and (b) Urbis.
▶ Explain that, as a major city at the centre of a conurbation, Manchester is at the top of the hierarchy of settlements. It has many functions and offers many services. Because it is at the top, there are few cities of its size in the UK and they are spread out across the country – Birmingham, Leeds, Glasgow and Newcastle-upon-Tyne are examples.
▶ Ask the children about visits they have made to major cities or, if they live in a city, visits to the city centre. How frequent are these visits? Why have they visited a city centre?

Activities
▶ Ask the children to record the characteristics of a large city to distinguish it from a town, for example it has major public buildings such as a cathedral and museums.
▶ Using a website such as www.bbc.co.uk/manchester, ask the children to plan a day visit to Manchester, or a similar city, to meet the needs of a family with disparate interests, for example a father who enjoys shopping for clothes, a mother who enjoys visiting art galleries and a son or daughter who is interested in science and technology.
▶ Although it is now a large city, Manchester had its origins as a Roman fort and settlement called Mamucium. It was at a strategic position on the route between the two major legionary fortresses at Chester (Deoua) and York (Eboracum). Ask the children to make a list of all the reasons why Manchester may have grown into a large city, for example it is at a crossroads of trade routes, it is on a river, it has plentiful flat land for building. The list will be a collection of positive site factors and will be a useful assessment of children's understanding of site and growth factors.

SETTLEMENTS

Conurbation

This image shows a conurbation – a major city surrounded by urban districts. A conurbation is formed when a city and neighbouring towns expand together and coalesce to form one continuous settlement. In the UK there are eight conurbations in which nearly 35% of the population live – the West Midlands, Greater Manchester, West Yorkshire, Glasgow, Merseyside, South Yorkshire, Tyne & Wear and Greater London.

The picture gives a good sense of how large settlements can spread to take in almost all available land in a locality – the limits of this conurbation appear to be the hills in the background. In the foreground, a major city can be seen with office blocks and other tall buildings at the centre. Low-rise buildings, including homes and shops, surround the centre and extend away into the distance. There is evidence of other high-rise buildings at some points in the distance – these indicate overspill estates and smaller towns that have become part of the conurbation as the urban sprawl has developed. Green spaces are relatively few in number and the picture gives a sense of relentless development.

Around many towns and cities in the UK there are areas of land which are protected from development. These 'green belt' areas cannot be built upon, which means that infill developments between settlements are less likely to occur than in the past. Conurbations centred on major cities are few in number in the UK (because they are at the top of a settlement hierarchy) and the cities at their centres have extensive spheres of influence (they serve a large number of settlements).

Discussing the photograph
▶ Discuss the human and physical features visible in the picture. Point out, in particular, the high-rise buildings in the foreground and at points in the distance, the sprawling housing developments, the few green spaces and the distant hills which provide a limit to the settlement. Note that the landscape is dominated by human features, as this is a large city surrounded by urban districts – known as a conurbation.
▶ Discuss why this city has grown so extensively. Note the plentiful flat land suitable for building.
▶ Tell the children about 'green belt' areas and ask them to find any evidence in the photograph of green-belt areas that have not been built upon. How important do the children think areas like these are in a conurbation?

Activities
▶ Ask the children to make a chart recording the similarities and differences between the conurbation and the school locality. If the school locality is part of a conurbation, the children can record where it is – is it part of the main city or in one of the surrounding urban areas?
▶ Ask the children to use a map of the UK to identify the eight major conurbations. Ask them to identify other cities that will have large spheres of influence (for example Bristol, Edinburgh and Belfast).
▶ Greater London is the largest conurbation in Western Europe with a population of over seven million (12 per cent of the UK population). This is relatively small, however, compared to other world cities. The conurbation of Tokyo in Japan, for example, is home to 28 million people! Ask the children to use a world map to identify other major cities and conurbations in the world. Split the children into groups to find out more about some of the cities identified. They should focus their research on identifying reasons why the cities have grown.

Defensive site

Early settlers chose their settlement sites carefully, bearing in mind key site factors. In the case of old settlements, such as the one in the picture, geographers have identified eight key factors:
1. An adequate supply of drinking water nearby – usually supplied by a well, river or spring.
2. Not too much water – settlers avoided marshy or frequently flooded sites.
3. A bridging or fording point on a river – allowing quick escape if attacked as well as providing potential for growth as a crossroads for transport and trade.
4. The availability of wood – used for fuel and as a building material.

SETTLEMENTS

5. The availability of stone for building – a nearby craggy hillside made up of an easily worked rock (such as sandstone, limestone or slate) could be a decisive influence on the choice of a settlement's location.
6. Flat land – building on a gradient could be difficult and therefore early settlers tended to settle on low-lying land as well as flat hilltops or plateaux.
7. Protection – early settlements were often founded in troubled times when protection from attack was a decisive factor. A hilltop site offered a vantage point to watch for attack and could be easily defended if an enemy approached.
8. Shelter from the weather – a south-facing aspect was better for agricultural land. As an easily defended site usually lacked shelter and a sheltered site could be open to attack, the choice of a settlement site would be a compromise between these different imperatives.

The picture shows a settlement where two site factors are clearly evident – protection and a bridging point on a river. The settlement is Kufstein in the Austrian Tyrol and the picture shows the city's fortress towering above a bridge over the River Inn. The fortress was first documented in 1205, although it was built much earlier than this, and the city grew up around the base of the rocky outcrop on which it was built. The fortress provided a place of refuge in time of war and guarded the bridging point over the river. Similar settlements can be found in the UK (for example, Alnwick in Northumberland or Stirling in Scotland), though few have factors so clearly evident.

Discussing the photograph

▶ Ask the children if they think this is a location in the UK. If not, why not? Explain that this is a place in a mountainous area of Austria, in Central Europe. Ask the children to find Austria on a map of Europe. (Kufstein is unlikely to be marked on a map of Europe because of its relatively small size.)
▶ Discuss and list the physical and human features in the photograph. How are they linked? (Castle on rocky outcrop, bridge over river.)
▶ Compare the physical and human features to those in the school locality. How are the buildings similar/different? How is the landscape similar/different?
▶ Why do the children think the castle/fortress was built on the site in the picture?
▶ Can the children see any other reasons why settlers may have chosen this place for a settlement? (Bridging point of river, fresh water provided by river, wood from the forests.)
▶ Tell the children about the eight factors considered by early settlers. Talk about the children's own locality and identify any factors that may be evident – for example, is there a river close by? Are houses built of local stone? Is there a defensive site nearby?

Activities

▶ Make a class concept map showing links between the human and physical features and reasons for a settlement on this site.
▶ Remind the children about the eight key site factors. Explain that some of these site factors may no longer be evident when visiting a settlement today or looking at it on a modern map – for example, forests that provided the supply of wood for a settlement may now have disappeared. Using a 1:50,000 scale OS map of your area, ask the children to work in groups to identify possible site factors for given selection of settlements on the map. (You should select old settlements for this activity.)

OS Map of Kelso, Kelso Town Hall

Site factors (as described in the previous section) describe the reasons why settlements were founded in particular locations by early settlers. However, site factors do not necessarily indicate why some settlements have flourished and developed and others have not. For example, Iron Age hill forts (built between 600 BC and AD 50), such as British Camp in the Malvern Hills in Herefordshire, were founded on relatively flat hilltops for good defensive reasons but were subsequently abandoned because other site factors such as lack of shelter and access to water counted against them. The possibility of expansion is key to a settlement's success and hill forts were also uniquely unsuitable for outward growth and development.

Most early settlements that have survived and flourished into the present day were built in valleys, usually on a river or stream. The factors involved in the choice of site would have included water supply, a bridging point and/or a sheltered aspect. The reasons for growth,

SETTLEMENTS

however, although linked to these factors, will have been different. A settlement in a valley will have grown because the river could be used for transport; land will have been easy to build on and have had room for expansion; the valley floor will have provided an easier route for roads, and later railways, to connect the settlement to other areas; good communications will have attracted industries and the settlement will have provided services for the surrounding area. Successful and growing settlements will have acquired certain features as they have grown over time – these could include a church, a market square, inns or public houses, a post office, shops, and/or housing estates.

The map shows Kelso, a small town in the Scottish Borders. Kelso provides a particularly good example of a place that was attractive to early settlers. A bridging point on a bend in a river offered defence on three sides. It has also adapted and changed to meet different needs over time – it is at a crossroads, is the site of an abbey, a castle, watermills and, in modern times, is the location for a racecourse, a secondary school and a hospital. The photograph shows the small, but rather grand town hall in the centre of Kelso on the market square.

Discussing the images

▶ Ask the children to look for and identify features in and around this settlement. What physical features can they identify? Discuss why early settlers may have initially chosen this site.
▶ Talk about the reasons why settlements grow and expand and ask the children why they think this settlement has grown.
▶ What evidence can the children see of different features from different times?
▶ As on all Ordnance Survey maps, some features are shown by symbols. Ask the children what the symbols tell them about Kelso. How many churches can they see? Can they spot a clue that Kelso is in a hilly area?
▶ Would the children like to live in this settlement? Why? Why not?
▶ Explain that the large building in the photograph is Kelso Town Hall. Ask the children to locate it on the map. They may need to be told that the OS abbreviation for Town Hall is TH.

Activities

▶ Ask the children to make a chart listing Kelso's site factors and reasons for growth.
▶ Ask them to sort the features shown on the map of Kelso into older and newer features and to explain why they think the features are old or new. They could then place the features on the map of Kelso on a timeline. Kelso is first mentioned in church documents in the 12th century, but was probably founded much earlier. The timeline need not show dates.
▶ Ask the children to work in groups to create a maps of a fictitious settlement. The settlement should show at least two significant site factors as well as features from different times – for example, a Roman fort, a castle, an abbey, a church, a factory, modern housing estate and a school. The children should use Ordnance Survey symbols to show features on their maps. Information sheets showing standard symbols can be found at www.ordnancesurvey.co.uk/education.

Place names

This map shows an area of Great Britain where there is evidence of place names with origins that derive from the languages of different groups of early settlers. It shows north-west Cheshire, the Wirral and north-west Wales. The place names in the west are representative of the languages spoken by the Celtic tribes that inhabited Britain before the Roman conquest in AD 43 – these names have survived because the area was not dominated by later settlers. These place names probably denote the earliest settlements on the map and are characterised by Welsh elements, such as 'Llan' meaning church, 'Bryn' meaning hill and 'Mynydd' meaning mountain.

Although the Romans were a significant group of settlers who took control by invasion, there is only one place name on the map with a Roman link – Chester's name derives from 'ceaster', an Old English word for a Roman town or city. To the Romans, Chester was the legionary fortress of 'Deva' or 'Deoua'. In the east of the map and on the Wirral, the place names derive from the languages of the two groups of early settlers who came after the Romans – the Anglo-Saxons and the Vikings.

From the late 4th century onwards (and hastened by the withdrawal of the Roman legions in AD 410) southern and central England was settled by tribes from what is now northern

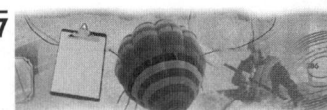

Germany – the Angles and the Jutes. The native Britons were driven north and west. A failed attempt to drive the settlers back by hiring mercenaries from another Germanic tribe – the Saxons – led to even more settlement and the map displays strong evidence of settlements founded by the Saxons. These place names have Saxon (later known as 'Old English') elements: notably 'ham' and 'ton' as suffixes – both meaning village or manor.

Evidence of the final group of early settlers (before the Norman invasion in 1066) can be seen in Wirral place names. These settlers came from Scandanavia, from AD 787 onwards, and were known as Norse, Danes or Vikings. Their settlements have place names with elements such as 'by' (meaning farm or village) or 'thing' (meaning a meeting place).

Two place names on the map are worthy of note: Wallasey is an Old English name meaning 'Island of the Welsh' and refers to this area in the north of the Wirral being an island in the past and a refuge for people of Celtic origin. Thingwall in central Wirral means 'a meeting place for an assembly' and indicates where a regional Viking assembly or parliament met. (The 'Tynwald' or parliament on the Isle of Man derives from the same Viking origin.)

Discussing the photograph

▶ Ask the children if they can find the area shown on this map on a map of the British Isles. The map shows parts of two countries in the United Kingdom. Which two?

▶ Distribute the 'Place names' photocopiable and explain to the children that one way of identifying early settlements, and who settled in different places, is to look closely at place names.

▶ Ask the children to identify place names on the map with the different elements shown on the photocopiable. Explain that the order on the handout is chronological. Ask the children to identify Celtic/Welsh, then Roman, then Saxon, then Viking place names.

▶ Ask the children if there are areas on the map where certain types of place names are more common.

▶ Ask them to suggest reasons why the oldest place names are in Wales and the Viking place names are closer to the coast. (The hilly terrain in Wales was a refuge for the Celtic people and did not attract later settlers; Viking settlers came by sea, so were likely to settle in sites close to the coast.)

Activities

▶ Print out copies of the map and ask the children to work in groups to make charts listing place names in the different settler categories – Celtic/Welsh, Roman, Saxon and Viking.

▶ Although the map does not show all the settlements in this area, it provides a fair reflection of the distribution of place names. Ask the children to identify the most common place names in different areas of the map, for example Wales, the Wirral and Cheshire. They can then colour in the map to show areas that appear to have been settled by the different settler groups. Which early settlers appear to have spread furthest?

NOTES ON THE PHOTOCOPIABLE PAGES

Word cards — PAGES 50–51

These cards contain some of the basic and more advanced vocabulary for the children to learn and use when looking at settlements. Read through the word cards with the children to familiarise them with the key words of the unit. Ask which words the children have heard before and clarify any they don't understand.

Activities

▶ Shuffle the cards and spread a set of cards on each group's table. Ask the children to find specific words you call out.

▶ Use the cards as a word bank to help the children label pictures and to help them with longer pieces of writing.

▶ Begin a glossary with the words and include any other topic vocabulary used in the unit.

SETTLEMENTS

Settlement pyramid
PAGE 52

This photocopiable shows a conventional settlement hierarchy diagram, used by geographers to differentiate between settlements of different types. The sectioned triangle or pyramid shape is used to indicate the number of settlements of each type in an area NOT the size of the settlements. The smallest section at the top indicates that there will only be one capital city, while the largest section indicates that there will be numerous farms.

Activities
▶ Introduce the children to the hierarchy of settlements diagram and explain that the size of the different sections indicates the number of that type of settlement in a locality.
▶ Ask the children to locate the hill farm on the diagram. Ask them to explain why they think the farm is at the base of the pyramid.
▶ As the children complete work on each type of settlement – hamlet, village, small town, market town, city, conurbation – locate it on the settlement diagram. For example, Hawkshead will go in the village section, Chester in the city section and Manchester in the conurbation city section.
▶ Print out photographs of the farm, hamlet, village, market town, city and conurbation from the CD. Make a display linking the images to their places in the settlement hierarchy diagram.

Place names and their origins
PAGE 53

This photocopiable lists some common prefixes, suffixes and words found in place names, grouped chronologically according to different groups of early settlers – Celts, Romans, Saxons and Vikings. It is designed to be used with the 'Place names' resource, which shows place names from all the settler groups, but can also be used to identify the origins of place names in the locality of the school.

Activities
▶ Use the photocopiable to help identify the origins of place names shown in the 'Place names' resource. Make a chart listing place names on the map in chronological order of settlement.
▶ Using a 1:50,000 OS map and the photocopiable, ask the children to identify the main group of early settlers that settled in their locality. Is there evidence, from place names, of several different groups of early settlers or were the school locality and surroundings settled only by one group?
▶ Explain to the children that place names are made up of words in old languages that describe the features of places. Using a 1:50,000 OS map of the area around the school's locality, ask the children to create new place names for places that they know in the vicinity based on the features of the places now. Encourage them to be creative, for example place names could be changed to 'Lotsofshops', 'Busyroad', 'Prettyview' or 'Noisyplace'.

Settlement word cards

SETTLEMENTS

| site |
| hamlet |
| village |
| market town |
| town |
| city |
| conurbation |

Settlement word cards

settlement
settler
aspect
bridging point
protection
place of worship
Celtic
Saxon
Viking

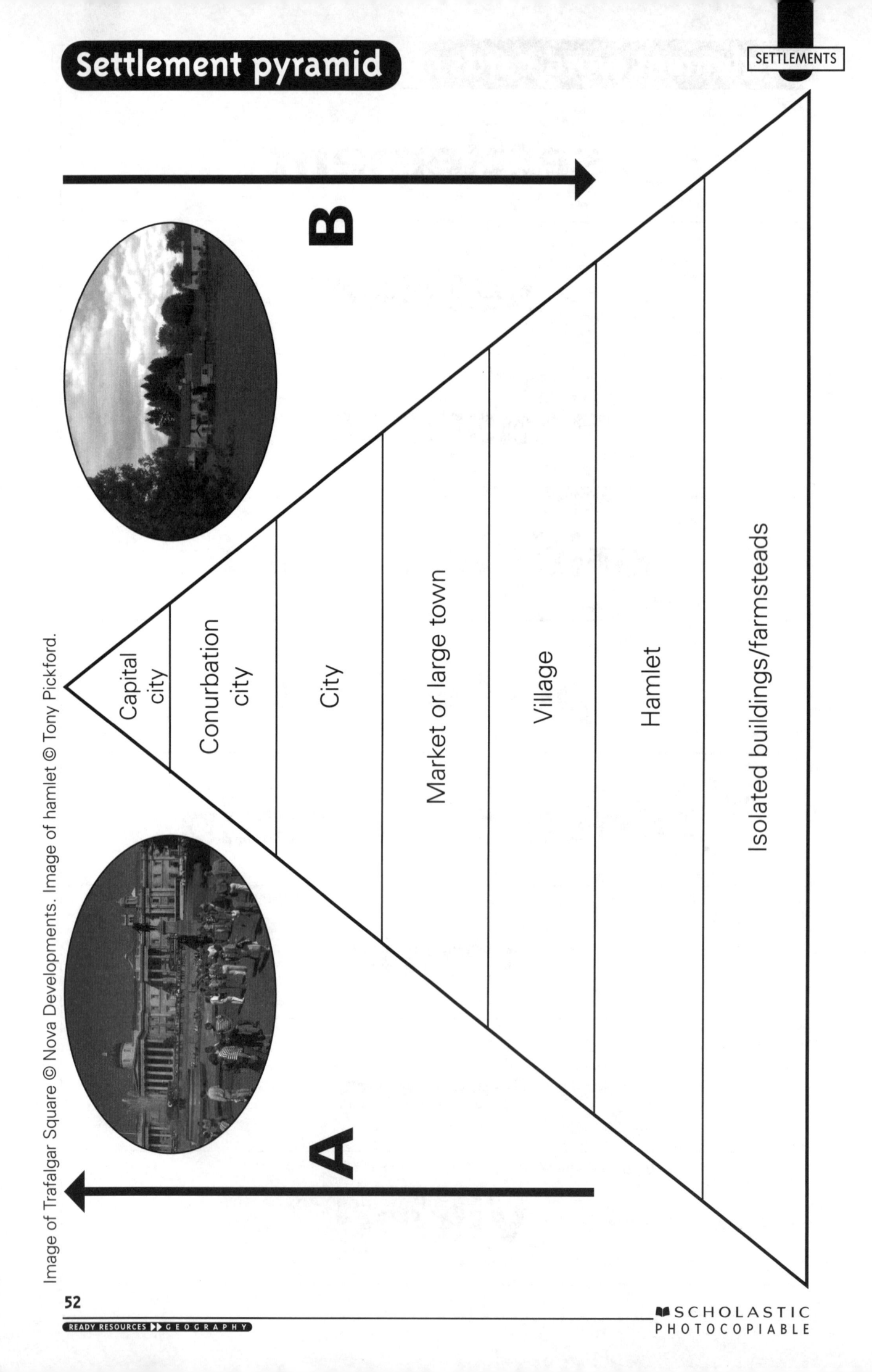

Settlement pyramid

SETTLEMENTS

A ←

B →

- Capital city
- Conurbation city
- City
- Market or large town
- Village
- Hamlet
- Isolated buildings/farmsteads

Image of Trafalgar Square © Nova Developments. Image of hamlet © Tony Pickford.

52

READY RESOURCES ▶▶ GEOGRAPHY

SCHOLASTIC PHOTOCOPIABLE

Place names and their origins

- One way of identifying early settlements and who settled in different places is to look closely at place names on a map.
- Listed below are some common prefixes, suffixes and words found in place names, grouped according to the different groups of settlers.

Celtic/Welsh		Saxon/Old English	
afon	river	*ham*	village
bryn	hill	*ton*	village
caer	fort		
mynydd	mountain	**Viking**	
moel	hill	*by*	farm
llan	church	*mere*	sandbank
pen	top	*thing*	meeting place
Roman			
Chester	town		

- Here are the meanings of some specific place names:

Helsby: village on a ledge – this settlement is on a hillside above the river Mersey.

Thingwall: field where an assembly meets – this was the location of a Viking parliament on the Wirral.

Wallasey: island of the Welsh – this was an island in the past and was the last place (in England) inhabited by the Celtic people who lived in the Wirral before the Saxons and Vikings came.

CONTRASTING LOCALITIES IN INDIA

Content and skills
The content of this chapter supports, augments and extends the activities in Unit 10 of the QCA Scheme of Work for geography, 'A Village in India' – a unit that aims to develop children's ideas about a locality in a less economically developed country (LEDC). The unit uses ActionAid's *Chembakolli* photo pack as an exemplar of how to carry out a study of a distant place, although it makes clear that the approaches could be used with other materials. The *Chembakolli* pack is now supported by other materials including a CD-ROM, storybooks and a dedicated website (www.chembakolli.com) – and, together, they make a compelling resource.

This chapter supports the unit by providing additional resources relating to southern India and the issue of deforestation. It augments and extends the unit by providing resources that give an impression of the diversity of India's landscapes, culture and human features. The resources in this section aim to enrich a locality study by conveying a sense of the variety and richness of India as a whole and not focusing exclusively on rural lives and issues. The study of any specific locality, similar in size to a school's locality in the UK, is unlikely to convey this diversity. The chapter will help you to meet the key National Curriculum requirement that children should, in their study of localities and themes, 'study at a range of scales – local, regional and national'.

Resources on the CD-ROM
The resources include photographs of a range of places and landscapes in the Indian sub-continent from the mountain ranges of the north to the tropical beaches of the south. Photographs of urban India are provided to balance those of undeveloped and rural landscapes. There are images showing transport, 'wild' habitats and high mountains. Some photographs touch on the issues of environmental change and sustainability. There is a map of India showing physical features and major settlements and a chart showing contrasting climates in different parts of India.

Photocopiable pages
The photocopiable pages in the book are also provided in PDF format on the CD-ROM and can be printed from there. They include:

▶ word cards containing essential vocabulary for the unit
▶ an activity sheet exploring the impact of Indian languages on the English language
▶ cards to support debates on the issue of deforestation.

Geographical skills
Using the resources and activities in this chapter will develop children's ability to read and interpret maps, graphs and charts and to identify key features within visual images. The activities will also support the development of geographical vocabulary.

CONTRASTING LOCALITIES IN INDIA

NOTES ON THE CD-ROM RESOURCES

Map of India

India is a vast country, with an area of 3.28 million square km (compared to the UK's 244,820 square km). Its landscapes, culture and human features are extremely diverse. This map shows the location of major physical features such as the Himalayas and the River Ganges and key human features such as the capital city of Delhi and other major settlements. Note that the map shows some recent changes to place names in India – Bombay, for example, is now named Mumbai. These changes reflect pronunciation and spelling in local languages.

Discussing the photograph
▶ List the physical features shown on the map and discuss their location. For example, where are the highest mountain ranges? Where are the main rivers? What other water features are labelled on the map?
▶ Ask the children to identify the capital city. How is it shown on the map? Are all the other places on the map towns and cities?
▶ Ask the children to identify the neighbouring countries that are labelled on the map.

Activities
▶ Ask the children what they know about India. What words would they use to describe their impressions of the country? Where have these impressions come from? From TV news? From books? From personal or family experience?
▶ What would the children expect to find if they visited India? Invite them to make predictions about climate and landscapes in Mumbai, Delhi or Kolkata.
▶ Use a globe or world map to locate and compare India to the British Isles. Ask the children to compare the sizes of the two countries and, if the globe or map shows physical features, ask them to predict what the landscape might be like in the north of India and in other areas.
▶ Working in groups, ask the children to list the countries that would be crossed on a flight to India, using a globe to help them. They should then do the same for an overland trip and record both routes to India on an outline world map.

Climate chart: Two Indian locations

The purpose of this chart is to convey some of the diversity of India through a comparison of climate in two different places. Srinigar is the summer capital of the state of Jammu and Kashmir in northern India. It lies at 1600m above sea level. It is a resort, criss-crossed by waterways and wooden bridges, with numerous mosques, palaces, a fortress and public gardens. Chennai (formerly known as Madras) is an industrial port on the Bay of Bengal and capital of the state of Tamil Nadu in southern India. It has a population of more than four million people. The two places are 2970km apart.

Srinigar's climate is temperate with a warm summer and cool winter. It has relatively low rainfall, with most occurring in the late winter months. In contrast, Chennai has a tropical climate. Mean temperatures are relatively high throughout the year, with little variation from summer to winter. Rainfall shows evidence of the monsoon – the wind pattern that brings seasonally heavy rain to South Asia. In winter, rainfall is negligible, but from the summer into the autumn, storms bring very heavy rainfall which can lead to extensive flooding.

Discussing the chart
▶ Before showing the chart, locate Srinigar and Chennai on the map of India (provided on the CD).
▶ On a world map or globe point out that Chennai is closer to the Equator than Srinigar and that Srinigar is in the north of India, in the foothills of the Himalayas.
▶ Ask the children to predict the climates of the two places. Which place would they expect to have a tropical climate (warm throughout the year with periods of heavy rainfall)? Which place would they expect to have a climate more like the UK?
▶ Display the chart and explain the meaning of the term 'mean temperature'. Ask the children to identify how the mean temperature and rainfall are shown on the chart.

▶ Ask the children to look at the lines showing mean temperature in the two places. How are the lines different? Note that the mean temperature of Srinigar never reaches that of Chennai.

▶ How would the children describe the pattern of mean temperatures in Chennai and Srinigar? Would they expect two places in the UK to be so different in terms of mean temperature? Why not?

▶ Ask the children to look at the bar chart showing monthly rainfall. How are the patterns of rainfall different in the two places? Ask the children to describe the pattern of rainfall in Chennai. Explain that Chennai's climate is dominated by the monsoon, which brings heavy rainfall in late summer and autumn.

▶ Show the children the chart which shows rainfall in Manchester in the UK ('Climate chart: Innsbruck and Manchester' from the chapter 'A European locality: the Tyrol' – available on the CD). Point out that, although the pattern of mean temperatures in Srinigar is comparable to the UK, the amount of rainfall is much lower. Around 200mm of rain falls in the wettest month in Manchester compared to 450mm in the wettest month in Chennai. Ask the children what might result from so much rain coming in a relatively short space of time.

Activities

▶ Tell the children to imagine that they are packing a small suitcase for a visit to Srinigar or Chennai. Ask them to identify ten items they would pack at different times of year for example January, August and October. When and where would they need, for example, warm clothes, waterproofs, sun block?

▶ If your study of India takes place during the autumn term, look for news items in newspapers and on the television news relating to the effects of monsoon rain in the Indian sub-continent. You can also access daily and weekly weather records and forecasts for Chennai and Srinigar at websites such as www.bbc.co.uk/weather. Compare weather data to data gathered in the school locality and ask the children to use data handling software to produce charts comparing weather conditions over a week, fortnight or month.

Market in Kerala

This photograph shows a market in the hill town of Munnar in southern India. Munnar is located in the Idukki district of the state of Kerala, west of Tamil Nadu. It lies 1520 metres above sea level. The word 'Munnar' means three rivers and the settlement is located at the meeting point of three streams. During the period of British rule in India, government officials went to Munnar in the summer to escape the stifling heat of the cities. There are about 30 tea plantations in and around Munnar and the tea estates are the town's main employers. The green hills in the background of the picture are part of the tea estates. Tea picking is still a highly labour-intensive industry with three crops of young leaves being plucked from the bushes by hand each summer.

The main focus of the picture is the neatly presented, colourful market stall with its range of fruit and vegetables. In the background is a busy hardware shop. The scene is comparable to similar scenes in market squares in the UK and confounds the stereotypical view that food is not plentiful in economically developing countries. The image suggests that Munnar is a thriving community and that the stallholder is expecting large numbers of shoppers.

Discussing the photograph

▶ Ask the children what they can see in the photographs. Make a list of the physical and human features shown.

▶ Have the children ever been to a place like this in or near the school's locality? How was it similar/different to this place?

▶ What items do the children recognise on the market stall? Which fruit and vegetables on this stall would they expect to find on a stall in a local market or in a local supermarket?

▶ What other shops or stalls can the children see? What does the sign above the shop in the background say? What would they expect to find in a hardware shop?

Activities

▶ Ask the children to make a list of the fruit and vegetables that they recognise in the picture. Some will probably be unfamiliar to them. If your school is in a large town or city, it may be possible to visit a shop that sells fruit and vegetables imported from India. You can

CONTRASTING LOCALITIES IN INDIA

then ask the shop owner to identify unfamiliar items. Alternatively, you could arrange to visit a wholesale fruit and vegetable market where the children will find a vast range of fresh foods imported from the Indian sub-continent for shops in local communities.

▶ Finding out the countries of origin of the foods that we eat is an effective way of illustrating the idea of global interdependence. Ask the children to collect food labels showing countries of origin – tinned food labels and labels from packs of fresh fruit and vegetables are ideal. Locate the countries of origin on a world map. Which food has travelled furthest? Are there any foods that come from Asia? If we only ate foods from the UK, which foods would children miss most? Emphasise that many everyday foods (such as bananas and oranges) and drinks (such as tea and coffee) cannot be produced in the UK, so we depend on countries like India for some of the staple foods in our diet.

Source of the River Ganges

This photograph shows the end or mouth of the Gangotri glacier in the Himalayas in the far north of India, close to the border with Tibet. It conveys the harsh, barren, snow-covered landscape of this region and provides a stark contrast to other images discussed in this chapter. The glacier is one of several in the high Himalayas and is a 24km river of ice, which remains permanently frozen. (More information on glaciers can be found in the chapter 'A European locality: the Tyrol'.) A stream flowing from a cave of ice at the mouth of the glacier is considered to be the source of the River Ganges.

The Ganges (or Ganga Mai meaning 'Mother Ganges') is the main river in India. Its course takes it across northern India from the Himalayas to the Bay of Bengal, where its mouth forms a huge delta – the largest estuarine delta in the world. The Ganges is 2510km long with two major tributaries – the Jumna and the Brahmaputra. The Jumna joins the Ganges at the city of Allahabad and the Brahmaputra joins at its delta in Bangladesh.

The River Ganges is considered to be holy by all Hindu people and bathing in the river is an important ritual. At Allahabad and Varanasi, temples crowd the riverbanks and steps, or ghats, lead down to the water. Pilgrims go down the steps to bathe or to fill bottles with the holy water. This has become a dangerous practice as the Ganges suffers from industrial pollution throughout its lower reaches. The river remains a vital source of water for northern India, however, with irrigation canals enabling crops, such as cotton and sugar cane, to be grown throughout the Ganges valley.

As the source of a holy river, the Gangotri glacier is also a pilgrimage site for Hindus. Many follow a pilgrimage trail from the nearby town of Gangotri over boulders, moraines and scree to Gaumukh ('the Cow's Mouth') to bathe in the river at the point where it issues from the glacier.

Discussing the photograph

▶ Ask the children to list the human and physical features in the picture. Can they see any human features? Why not?
▶ What words would the children use to describe the landscape in the picture?
▶ Do the children know the names of any mountains in the Himalayas? (Examples include Mount Everest, K2 and Kanchenjunga.)
▶ Tell the children that the picture shows the Himalayan mountain range at a point over 3000m above sea level. Explain that the feature in the centre of the picture is a glacier – and that the water that issues from it is the source of the River Ganges. Point out the Ganges on the map of India and explain that the Ganges is a holy river to Hindus. Ask the children why they think the place shown in the photograph is important in India.

Activities

▶ Ask the children to make a sketch of the image and annotate it with appropriate labels such as glacier, mountain peaks, snow, the source of the River Ganges, rocks, boulders.
▶ As a class, make a list of words to describe the landscape in the photograph and another list to describe the landscape in a contrasting place in India, such as the Kanha National Park.
▶ Use the internet to find images showing the Ganges at other points in its course and challenge the children to match the images to points on the map.
▶ Gaumukh is a popular destination for backpackers as well as pilgrims. Ask the children to use evidence in the image to write an imaginative diary entry for a backpacker entitled 'My visit to Gaumukh'.

CONTRASTING LOCALITIES IN INDIA

Tiger in Kanha National Park

Established as a protected area in 1955, the Kanha National Park is in the state of Madhya Pradesh in the central highlands of India. Spread out over an area of 940 square km, it is situated in a valley where forests, intermingled with characteristic grassland or savannah areas (as shown in the photograph), cover large tracts of land. Kanha is home to 22 species of mammals including tigers, deer, Indian bison and wild dogs. It was the inspiration for Rudyard Kipling's *Jungle Book*.

Kanha was a noted tiger-hunting ground prior to the establishment of the National Park. A conservation project, named 'Project Tiger', was set up in 1972 to save the area's big cats from extinction. It has been highly successful and the number of tigers in Kanha has doubled to more than 100. Tiger conservation is not an easy task; tigers are at the top of the food chain (preyed on only by human poachers) and, for them to flourish, their prey must be protected too.

Because of the success of 'Project Tiger', Kanha is one of the best places in India for viewing tigers in the wild. It is a popular tourist destination, featuring on the itineraries of many tour companies. To minimise disturbance to wildlife, Kanha has a core zone, which is not visited by tourists, and a tourist zone where visitors have an opportunity to see tigers while travelling in four-wheel drive vehicles or on the backs of elephants.

Discussing the photograph

▶ Explain to the children that this type of open grassland with a few trees is called savannah. Tigers prefer this type of landscape for hunting their prey. Can the children think why?
▶ Discuss what words the children would use to describe the landscape and make a list.
▶ Find Kanha National Park on the map of India and ask the children to describe it in relation to other places.
▶ The photograph was taken in the tourist zone of the National Park. What do the children think happened before the picture was taken? What do they think happened after the picture was taken?

Activities

▶ Ask the children to make a chart comparing the landscape of the Kanha National Park with another location in India such as the Himalayas.
▶ Set the children the task of finding out about the range of animals that live in the Kanha National Park or in a similar tiger reserve using reference books or appropriate websites. They could then construct a food web for the habitat.
▶ There is pressure on tiger reserves to allow greater access by tourists. Ask the children to complete one of the following tasks: (a) write a persuasive letter from a tour company to the Director of Kanha asking for greater access to the reserve, (b) write a response from a wildlife ranger arguing that access should be reduced to protect the wildlife or (c) create a poster promoting the attractions of Kanha to responsible tourists.

Gateway of India in Mumbai

Mumbai is a city and industrial port on the west coast. It is the capital of the state of Maharashtra and one of India's largest cities, with a population of more than 18 million people. Previously known as Bombay, the city was renamed Mumbai in 1995. The main employers are the long-established industry of cotton textiles and the more modern industries of motor vehicle manufacture, electronics, and papermaking. Mumbai is also the centre of the Indian film industry – sometimes known as 'Bollywood'.

Mumbai's climate is similar to that of Chennai – it is hot and humid throughout the year with heavy rainfall during the monsoon season. The combination of sticky heat, heavy traffic and millions of people going about their daily lives makes Mumbai a hectic, vibrant place, characterised by noise, pollution and the smell of spicy food. The area of Mumbai shown in the photograph is one of the few places where residents and visitors can escape the hustle and bustle by taking a cruise around the harbour. Three cruise boats can be seen in the picture.

The grand arch, shown on the right of the photograph, provides a link to the colonial past. Known as the 'Gateway of India', the arch was built to commemorate the visit to India by

CONTRASTING LOCALITIES IN INDIA

King George V and Queen Mary in 1911. It opened in 1924 and was the scene, 25 years later, of the departure of the last regiment of British troops at the end of colonial rule. On the left is the Taj Mahal Hotel which was built at the height of British rule in 1903 and comprises a strange mix of architectural styles.

Discussing the photograph
▶ Ask the children to list words to describe the buildings in the picture. What tells them that these are special buildings?
▶ Discuss how the buildings are similar/different to buildings in the school locality. Is there anything in the picture that tells them that this is India and not the UK?
▶ What do the children think the boats in the picture are used for?
▶ Explain that the buildings in the picture were built on the waterfront at Mumbai at a time when the British governed India. Although colonial rule ended more than 50 years ago, India still has very strong links with Britain. Many people in Britain have family links to countries in the Indian sub-continent – Pakistan, Bangladesh and Sri Lanka, as well as India itself.

Activities
▶ As well as family links, there are other ways in which Indian culture influences every day life in the UK. For example, foods from the Indian sub-continent are very popular. Through discussion, identify any links between the school locality and India. These might be in the form of restaurants selling food from the sub-continent or place names. In Belfast, Blackburn, Manchester and London, for example, there are streets called 'Bombay Street'.
▶ Alongside the Taj Mahal, the 'Gateway of India' is a symbol of India that is known throughout the world. Ask the children to think of other landmarks that are symbolic of countries. Examples include the Eiffel Tower, the Pyramids, the Great Wall of China. What buildings or landmarks might people around the world associate with the UK? Ask the children to choose one of these landmarks and make a chart comparing it to the 'Gateway of India', using reference materials to help them.

Street in India, Video: Indian traffic

The photograph shows a street scene in Amritsar in the Punjab area of northern India. Amritsar is an industrial city of more than one million inhabitants and is the site of the Golden Temple, the most important sacred shrine to followers of the Sikh religion. The turbans worn by the men on the horse-drawn cart in the picture indicate that they are Sikhs.

The street scenes in the photograph and video give an impression of the range of transport found in urban and rural environments in India. They show motor transport (a parked motor scooter) and more traditional forms of transport – a horse-drawn cart and bicycle rickshaws used as taxis. The lack of cars, buses and lorries suggests that these are not common in India but this is an erroneous impression – India has a thriving motor manufacturing industry and, in 2002, there were more than 7.5 million private cars on Indian roads. In common with other economically developing countries, however, India has fewer cars for the size of population than the UK and everyday travel tends to be by other forms of transport.

Discussing the photograph and video
▶ Compare the street scenes to similar ones in the school locality and discuss the similarities and differences. Encourage the children to think about the forms of transport that they can see and whether or not these could be used in the school locality. They might also think about the different sounds that they might hear.
▶ Ask the children what they think the climate is like in these places. What time of year do they think the picture was taken? (The climate in Amritsar will be similar to that of Srinigar, as shown on the 'Climate chart' on the CD.)

Activities
▶ Ask the children to make a chart comparing transport in the street scene and transport in the school locality and then to write a list of the advantages and disadvantages of each form of transport. For example, a bicycle rickshaw taxi will be slower than a motor taxi, but will cause less pollution and may be quicker if streets are busy.
▶ Ask groups of children to brainstorm a list of words to describe the street scene. They should include words to describe the buildings, clothes and stalls on the street as well as transport.

CONTRASTING LOCALITIES IN INDIA

Video: Rush hour in India

This video clip shows rush hour in a street in the centre of Chennai. The use of time-lapse photography allows the street to be viewed over a long period of time. Children may be unfamiliar with this type of clip and may find it quite amusing, so it is important to show it several times before asking them to comment on it. The video shows large numbers of people on the move and examples of public transport (in the form of buses and taxis, the white vehicles on the left). There appear to be many small lorries and vans but relatively few private cars.

Like other Indian cities, Chennai has experienced a great deal of inward migration, with people moving from the countryside into the city to seek better education, better jobs and a higher standard of living. Such population movements have contributed to the high population density and sense of overcrowding in some cities. Most of the people seen in the clip will be moving to and from their places of work. Their jobs may be in Chennai's long-established industries, such as cotton textiles or bicycle manufacture, or in newer technology-based industries, such as call centres. Several large corporations, such as Citigroup Bank and Hewlett Packard, operate call centres in Chennai. It is possible that a telephone query made in the UK about a bank account or computer problem could be answered by someone in a Chennai call centre.

Discussing the video

▶ Ask the children what type of place this video clip shows. Do they think this is a city, town or village? Why do the people and traffic in the clip appear to be moving strangely? Explain that the clip has been made using time-lapse photography so that quite a long period of time is compressed into a short video.
▶ Discuss how the street is similar and different to streets in the school locality. Where might you find a street like this in the UK?
▶ What traffic can the children see on this street? What is the main form of transport they can see? How is this similar/different to a city street in the UK?
▶ What time of day do the children think it is? Why?

Activities

▶ Ask the children to make a list of words and phrases to describe the scene in the video clip. As well as listing transport types, they should find words to describe the sights and probable sounds of a place like this.
▶ Use the pause and step forward facility on the movie clip player to move through the video slowly. Taking one form of transport at a time (buses, taxis, lorries, vans, cars) make a tally of the traffic in the street.
▶ Ask the children to use data handling software to present a traffic survey of the street in Chennai. The children should then compare this to a traffic survey in the school locality and look for similarities as well as differences.

Tropical beach

The photograph shows a tropical beach, namely Palolem Beach in Goa, western India. Goa's beaches are fringed by palm trees and conjure up images of idyllic, 'desert island' lifestyles. The beaches attract many tourists to the region. Tourism is a significant industry in India, employing large numbers of people, but it also raises land-use issues. Remote beaches are under threat from hotel and leisure developments – and, by seeking out unspoilt beaches, visitors may contribute to the destruction of these fragile environments.

The other major industry on the coast is fishing. Most fishermen from Goa use traditional open boats to catch fish and prawns – and examples of these boats can be seen in the distance. Over-fishing in the Arabian Sea has recently become a problem and fishing is not allowed from May to July or August. This has led to protests from the fishing communities because of unemployment and lack of income during the summer.

Discussing the photograph

▶ Ask the children to discuss and list the physical and human features that can be seen in the picture.

CONTRASTING LOCALITIES IN INDIA

▶ Ask them what sounds they might be able to hear if they were in this place. What textures might they feel with their hands and feet? Would the children like to visit this place? Why? Why not?
▶ Why do the children think tourists come to visit a place like this? What would happen if too many came?

Activities
▶ Ask the children to make a chart comparing Palolem Beach to a beach location in the UK and to record what is similar and what is different.
▶ Challenge the children to write a radio advertisement to attract visitors to Goa and its beaches. They should target the people who come to India to see the Himalayas or the National Parks, rather than relax, swim and sunbathe on the beaches. How would the children persuade these visitors to come to Goa?
▶ Set up a role-play scenario in which a large company wants to build a hotel on this beach to attract more tourists. Divide the children into groups and ask each group to decide on the point of view of one of the following individuals or interest groups: a member of the local tourist board, an unemployed fisherman, an environmental campaigner, a visitor to Goa from the UK, the owner of a small hotel in a nearby village. Groups should report back on their viewpoints as part of a public enquiry into the project.

Railway station

Every day, India's railways carry an average of 12 million passengers and more than one million tonnes of freight traffic. The network covers 7058 stations and is spread over 62,725 square km. It is the world's largest railway network and Indian Railways (IR) is the largest employer in the world, with 1.6 million employees. Trains are the main form of transport for long distance travel in India because they are a relatively quick way of covering the vast distances on the sub-continent. Although the road structure is improving, the standard of the roads is still variable.

The standard of trains varies across the network. On major routes, there are air-conditioned expresses where meals are served. Local trains tend to be very basic and second-class travel on any train can mean sitting for long hours on wooden benches in cramped conditions. The network is also made up of different gauges of tracks which means that journeys can involve several changes.

Because the railways are so popular, the busy scene shown in the photograph is common. Urban stations are crowded places with large numbers of people embarking, disembarking or waiting for trains. The station in the picture is at Margao in the state of Goa, about 6km from the coast. Margao is the only station in the state served by long-distance rail services.

Discussing the photograph
▶ Discuss how the railway station is similar or different to the ones that the children have visited in the UK. Why do the children think railways are more popular in India than in the UK?
▶ Do the children think the people on the platform are waiting for a local or a long-distance train? What do the suitcases suggest? Notice that there appear to be several families waiting on the platform.
▶ Do they think people have been waiting for a long or a short time? Why?
▶ Ask the children to suggest words to describe the scene. Does this look like part of a small or a large railway station? (Note that the photograph shows a sign for Platform 16.)

Activities
▶ Ask the children to list reasons for people making journeys. For what reasons might people make journeys to and from Margao? (Note that the station is in Goa, a popular tourist area.)
▶ Like many other countries India has a great deal of internal migration with individuals and families moving from the countryside to cities to seek work and a higher standard of living. Ask the children to imagine that they are waiting on the station for a train that will take them to a city to live. Ask them to list words/phrases to describe their feelings. What might their hopes and concerns be?

READY RESOURCES ▶▶ GEOGRAPHY 61

Deforestation

This photograph displays evidence of significant environmental change in southern India – a phenomenon known as deforestation. It shows part of a forest where trees have been chopped down for fuel or to make way for farmland. India's growing population of 1.1 billion has put a great deal of pressure on the environment, especially in rural areas, and deforestation is one way in which the environment is being drastically changed by human intervention. It is estimated that 2.7 per cent of India's forests are destroyed each year.

Although new land for farming is much needed, the destruction of forests has had unintended but severe consequences. Once trees have been cut down, the soil that is exposed is poor and thin and unsuitable for long-term farming. In the rainforest areas of tropical India, monsoon rains wash the topsoil away and the resulting floods lead to further erosion. On sloping land, there are mudslides that can engulf small settlements. The process then leads to further destruction because the eroded farmland can only be replaced by cutting down more trees.

Deforestation damages biodiversity and threatens wildlife. It is also suggested that the destruction of forests has contributed to the increased severity of flooding caused by the monsoon across India and in Bangladesh. Because forests in Nepal and in the Ganges Valley have been destroyed, rainwater now runs quickly down bare hillsides and across deforested floodplains to fill rivers and make flooding deeper and more intense.

Discussing the photograph

▶ Ask the children what they think the photograph shows. What do they think has happened here? If nobody provides the right answer, explain that trees have been cut down from this land and that, now the trees have gone, there is nothing to stop the soil from being washed away by the monsoon rains.

▶ Ask the children why they think the trees have been cut down. What could this land be used for now?

Activities

▶ Working in pairs or groups, ask the children to write a list of reasons why cutting down forests is not a good idea.

▶ Demonstrate the process of erosion by using a watering can, with a rose attachment, to shower water onto a tray of sand. The water will wash out channels and rivulets like those in the picture. (Although it is not an entirely accurate representation, it will help the children to visualise what happens.) Repeat the experiment with another tray of sand, this time using fine netting to cover the sand. There should be less 'erosion', illustrating how tree roots protect the soil from being washed away. Compare the sand in the two trays.

▶ How would the children persuade an Indian farmer, who desperately needs more land to grow crops, not to cut down trees? Challenge them to write a short speech from the point of view of an environmental campaigner.

NOTES ON THE PHOTOCOPIABLE PAGES

Word cards   PAGES 64–65

These cards contain vocabulary for the children to learn and use when looking at contrasting localities in India. They include:
▶ names of places and physical features
▶ geographical terms relating to the subcontinent and to the themes covered in the chapter.

Read through the word cards with the children to familiarise them with the key words of the unit. Ask which words the children have heard before and clarify any they don't understand.

Activities

▶ Shuffle the cards and spread out a set of cards on each group's table. Ask the children to find specific words you call out.

CONTRASTING LOCALITIES IN INDIA

▶ Use the cards as a word bank to help the children label pictures and to help them with longer pieces of writing.
▶ Begin a glossary with the words and include any other topic vocabulary used in the unit.
▶ Ask the children to group the cards into words/places we know, words/places we think we know and words/places we would like to find out about. Make this into a display and, as children encounter the words, move them into the 'Words we know' section and add definitions, explanations or descriptions.

Indian words in English   PAGE 66

The English language owes a great deal to languages from the Indian sub-continent. Many everyday words originated in India – some, like curry and basmati, are obvious; others, like shampoo and cot, are less obvious. This sheet provides a small selection of the many words that have come into English from Indian languages.

Activities
▶ Working in pairs, challenge the children to match the words to their meanings, using a dictionary to help them if necessary.
▶ Ask the children to group the words into those they would have expected to come from India and words they did not expect to have an Indian origin.
▶ Set the children the task of finding other common words that have origins in another language. Foods provide a good starting point – for example pizza, croissant and yoghurt. Make the point that our language and culture is made richer by these 'foreign' words and the contributions of ethnic groups.

Deforestation debate   PAGE 67

Use this sheet to explore issues relating to deforestation in India. Encourage the children to discuss the activity together before making any decisions. It is important to make the point that, although to us deforestation seems a very bad idea, in India it is carried out for very good reasons.

Activities
▶ Working in groups, ask the children to cut out these cards and sort them into reasons for and against deforestation.
▶ When the children have identified reasons why deforestation should not take place, ask them to sort the reasons in order of importance. Which is the most important reason that trees should not be cut down? Which reasons are less important?
▶ Ask the children to design a poster for a campaign against deforestation in India, choosing no more than three key points.

India word cards

Amritsar
Chennai
Delhi
Ganges
Goa
Himalayas
Mumbai
Tamil Nadu

CONTRASTING LOCALITIES IN INDIA

India word cards

CONTRASTING LOCALITIES IN INDIA

monsoon
source
tiger
national park
deforestation
Hindu
Hindi
Sikh

Indian words in English

- The words below have all been borrowed from the languages of the Indian sub-continent. Match the words with their meanings.

Words	Meanings
anaconda	A raft made of logs, used now to describe a boat with two hulls
bangle	A large snake
bungalow	A tropical fruit with a thin skin and sweet yellow flesh
catamaran	A spicy sauce
cheetah	A sweet substance used in food and drinks
cot	A citrus fruit and the name of a colour
curry	A black and white animal
Himalaya	A bracelet
jungle	A member of the cat family that can run very fast
loot	A thick forest
mango	A place for a baby to sleep
orange	Stolen goods
panda	A name for a mountain range, which means 'Home of the Snow'
sari	A woman's dress made from a long piece of cloth that is wrapped around the body
sugar	A single-storey house

- Below are four more Indian words used in English. Use a dictionary to find out their meanings.

juggernaut   rogue   dungaree   veranda

CONTRASTING LOCALITIES IN INDIA

Deforestation in India

If the trees are removed, the unprotected soil is washed away in heavy monsoon rains.	After trees are cut down, heavy rain can quickly run down bare hillsides into rivers causing deep and severe floods.
Forests provide a habitat for plants and animals, especially endangered animals such as tigers.	Farmers need more land to grow crops and to feed animals.
Wood is needed for all sorts of purposes, from making paper to making furniture.	Villagers need cheap fuel to warm their homes in winter.
When forest trees are cut down and burned they release carbon dioxide, which pollutes the atmosphere and is believed to contribute to global warming.	Land is needed for hydro-electric schemes that make cheap electricity. Forests must be cut down to make way for reservoirs and dams.
The soil in forests is usually very thin and low in nutrients. After trees have been cleared, farmers can usually only grow crops for two or three years.	Tree roots hold soils together and slow down the flow of water in the monsoon season, reducing erosion and preventing flooding.

A EUROPEAN LOCALITY: THE TYROL

Content and skills
The Programme of Study for geography states that children should study 'at a range of scales – local, regional and national' and 'a range of places and environments in different parts of the world, including... the European Union'. This chapter will help you to meet these requirements by focusing on a locality in the Austrian province of the Tyrol. The locality is placed in its regional context – the Alps – and the landscape and lifestyles are explored through a range of resources.

There are substantial links to the QCA Scheme of Work for geography including Unit 15 'The mountain environment', Unit 13 'A contrasting UK locality: Llandudno' (the content provides a highly appropriate follow-up to a study of a traditional British seaside tourist resort) and Unit 16 'What's in the news?' (the possible impact of climate change on winter tourism).

The content of this chapter also aims to provide a self-contained unit, which will enable children to find out about the physical and human features of a place that is likely to contrast with their school locality. There are few places in the UK where there is the same combination of climate, tourist facilities, traditional agriculture and mountainous terrain as in the Tyrol. Using the resources, discussion points and activities in this chapter will also help to develop children's visual literacy skills and, specifically, their ability to gather information from images, maps and charts.

Resources on the CD-ROM
The resources include photographs and a video clip of a range of settlements in the Tyrol ranging from an isolated farm to a busy village with a tourist economy. There are photographs showing the Alpine landscape in summer and winter and photographs that help to convey the scale of this major European mountain range. Seasonal activities as well as aspects of everyday life are shown in the photographs and the Alpine climate is conveyed through images and a chart.

Photocopiable pages
The photocopiable pages in the book are also provided in PDF format on the CD-ROM and can be printed from there. They include:
▶ word cards containing essential vocabulary for the unit
▶ a newspaper article about the effects of climate change on the Alpine ski industry.

Geographical skills
Using the resources and activities in the chapter will develop the skills of map reading and interpretation, analysing and interpreting graphs and charts, identification of key features within visual images and the development of geographical vocabulary.

A EUROPEAN LOCALITY: THE TYROL

NOTES ON THE CD-ROM RESOURCES

Map of Austria

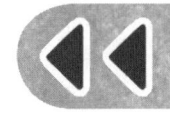

This map shows Austria and its provinces. The Tyrol is a mountainous province in western Austria, and lies at the eastern end of the Alps. Although the highest mountains lie to the west, parts of the Tyrol province are above the snowline, with peaks permanently covered in snow. The landscape is dominated by high mountains but the region is also characterised by forested, fertile valleys in which settlements have developed. Winter and summer tourism are strong factors in the province's economy but the Tyrol is also important for the production of hydroelectric power. Forestry is another major employer and there are industries producing gas-powered engines, machine tools and crystal glass.

Discussing the photograph
▶ Explain to the children that this map shows part of Austria. Find Austria on a map of Europe or the world. Can the children describe where Austria is in relation to the UK?
▶ What physical and human features can the children see on this map? How are these shown on the map?
▶ What place names can the children see? Which appear to be the larger settlements? Which settlement is the most important?
▶ What routes can the children see on the map? Where do the routes go to and from?

Activities
▶ Ask the children to make a chart listing human and physical features of the Austrian Tyrol. Record any links between human and physical features – for example, settlements appear to be in valleys, not in the mountains.
▶ Ask the children to predict what the landscape will be like in particular locations (for example, the mountains or in Innsbruck).
▶ Use travel planning websites to plan a trip to the Austrian Tyrol. Ask the children to identify the shortest, cheapest and most interesting routes and to list the countries that they would cross on a flight to Austria or on an overland trip.

FARMING IN THE TYROL

Tyrolean farmhouse

This photograph shows a farmhouse in north-east Tyrol. The farmhouse is characteristic of this area as it combines the farmer's living quarters, stables and barn under one roof. The balcony on the gable side of the house and the window boxes full of flowers are also familiar features. The number of windows to the front and side of the house indicate extensive living quarters. (In Austria, it is normal for several generations of a family to live together in one household.) Wood, which will be used for heating in winter, is stacked on the right of the building. The ramp on the right, leading to the barn, suggests that the first floor is used to store the farmer's equipment: tractors, trailers and grass-cutting machinery.

Agriculture in the Tyrol maintains traditional practices and has been heavily subsidised. The mountain farming cycle is governed by the seasons. In spring, cattle are led to high mountain pastures and in the autumn they return to farms on the lower slopes and in the valleys to be fed indoors through the harsh winter.

Discussing the photograph
▶ Ask the children to identify clues to the function of the building. What features suggest that this is a farm?
▶ Point out the two distinct parts of the building at the front and rear. Ask the children to identify the living quarters.
▶ Ask the children to list words to describe the building and its site. Does the farm appear to be high in the mountains or in a valley?
▶ Point out the quietness of the scene and the fact that the farm seems almost deserted. Ask the children why they think this is. (As this is high summer, the farmer's cows will be

A EUROPEAN LOCALITY: THE TYROL

on mountain pastures, not on the farm, and the farmer may be with them or out in his fields cutting grass for winter feed.)
▶ Tell the children that the wood is stacked behind the building. Why would the farmer use wood for winter fuel? (Note the forests in the background.) Why do we rarely use wood for this purpose in the UK?

Activities
▶ As a class, make a list of words to describe (a) the picture in general, (b) the farm building and (c) the site of the farm.
▶ Brainstorm words associated with the word 'farm', focusing on what farms and farmers do and different types of farm.
▶ Ask the children to list the similarities and differences between this farm building and a farm in the UK. The Farming and Countryside Education (FACE) website (www.face-online.org.uk) contains several farm profiles showing the characteristics of different types of farms in the UK.

Modern alm, Traditional alm

These images show high mountain farms or alms. These are used in the summer months when cows are brought to high mountain pastures for grazing. Although most of the cows are fattened over the summer for their meat, some are kept for their milk. The alms have small milking parlours and the cows are milked twice a day. The milk is produced in small quantities compared to a large dairy farm in the UK. The milk is highly valued because it is produced on unpolluted mountain slopes without the use of chemicals or fertilisers.

In the past, a farmer's life on an alm in summer could have been a lonely, isolated existence. Nowadays, modern vehicles and improved mountain roads mean that the alms are easily accessible. The clouds in the background of the traditional alm indicate the height of the location; the farmer's car shows that it is accessible by road. The modern alm is in a better condition and the signpost for walkers suggests that it is on a tourist trail.

Discussing the photographs
▶ Explain to the children that both alms are situated on flatter parts of high mountain slopes.
▶ Ask the children what time of year they think the pictures were taken (summer). Point out that these small mountain farms are only used in the summer months. Why would they not be used for grazing cows in winter?
▶ Ask the children to identify the animals in the pictures. Why do farmers keep cows?
▶ What differences between the two alms can the children see? Which alm do they think may be visited by tourists?

Activities
▶ Ask the children to list the physical and the human features in the images.
▶ Ask them to make a chart with the headings 'Summer' and 'Winter'. Using the picture to help them, they should describe how the alms appear in summer and suggest what they may be like in winter.

Alpine cows

This photograph shows cows grazing in an Alpine meadow in summer. Cows are the main livestock in mountain farms and most are raised for meat and fattened over the summer on high mountain pastures like this one. Since Austria joined the EU in 1995, mountain farmers have been encouraged to take on organic farming methods so that their products can be sold at higher prices – and mountain farmers in Austria tend to have far smaller herds than cattle farmers in the UK.

Some of the cows in the photograph have bells attached to collars around their necks. These are both functional and traditional. The cows are allowed to roam far and wide across the mountain slopes so the jangling bells enable the farmer to keep track of the herd. The bells have become a symbol of the Tyrol and miniature versions are sold in tourist shops as souvenirs. Larger versions can be heard ringing out during downhill ski races in the winter to encourage the Austrian competitors.

A EUROPEAN LOCALITY: THE TYROL

Discussing the photograph
▶ Ask the children what physical features they can see in the picture. What clues tell them that the cows are on a high mountain slope? What human features can be seen?
▶ What can the children see on the necks of some of the cows? Why do they think the cows wear bells?
▶ Note the chairlift in the background. Ask the children to describe what this place might be like in winter.

Activities
▶ As a class, list any advantages and disadvantages to the farmer of this type of cattle grazing.
▶ Mountain farms are uneconomic so it could be argued that they should be abandoned and agriculture concentrated in the lowlands, where the land is better and larger herds can be kept. Challenge the children to write a persuasive letter to a newspaper or Austrian government minister, arguing the case for maintaining mountain farms. They could include the following points in their argument: mountain farms are environmentally-friendly and produce better-quality milk; the farms attract tourists to the area; the cows maintain the landscape; without the farms, the pastures would become overgrown and unsightly.

Cutting grass

In the summer, Alpine farmers need to cut the grass to make hay and silage to feed cows indoors during the winter. The meadows lower down the mountainsides and in the valleys are used to grow several crops of grass for this purpose. On lowland farms in the UK, the cutting, drying and gathering of grass is a process carried out by heavy machinery pulled by tractors. In the Tyrol, tractors cannot be used because most meadows are on steep slopes. Instead, the farmers have to use hand tools, such as scythes, or small grass cutters like the one shown in the photograph.

In some ways, this machine is similar to a domestic lawnmower – it is steered from the rear and a small petrol engine drives the cutting blades. However, there is no grass box to gather the cuttings (the cut grass must be left to dry), the motor drives sideways cutting blades and there are four substantial wheels with thick treads.

Discussing the photograph
▶ Discuss the physical and the human features in the picture. Note the modern house in the background, possibly built as a holiday home to provide additional income for the farm.
▶ Ask the children what they think the machine in the picture is used for. How is it similar/different to a domestic lawnmower?
▶ Using clues in this and other pictures, ask the children to identify why this type of grass cutter will be used on an Alpine farm rather than larger machinery pulled by a tractor.
▶ What features on the grass cutter will make it (a) able to grip on a steep slope and (b) usable after dark?

Activities
▶ Ask the children to make a chart showing the cycle of an Alpine farmer's year – cattle indoors in winter, herds moved to high pastures in spring, cutting grass for hay and silage in summer, cattle brought back to lower slopes in autumn.
▶ Use the farm profiles on the Farming and Countryside Education (FACE) website (www.face-online.org.uk) to compare the chart to a UK hill farmer's year. What are the similarities and differences?

SKIING IN THE TYROL

Gondola leaving base, Gondola on mountain, Gondola station

These photographs show the Hoch Söll and Hohe Salve gondolas, which ascend and descend the Hohe Salve mountain near Söll. Originally built as a system to carry skiers in winter, the gondolas also operate during the summer to carry tourists and local families to high paths, viewpoints and mountain restaurants.

A EUROPEAN LOCALITY: THE TYROL

'Gondola leaving base' shows the bottom station of the Hoch Söll gondola. The busy car park provides an indication of the popularity of this lift on summer weekends. In the background the stark, rocky summits of the limestone Wilder Kaiser (Wild Emperor) mountains can be seen.

'Gondola on mountain' shows an ascending gondola near the top station of the Hohe Salve gondola. The clouds in the background give a clue to the height of the top station (1829m).

'Gondola station' shows a family disembarking from the Hoch Söll Gondola at the middle station, half way up the mountain. The Hohe Salve and Hoch Söll gondolas are linked at the middle station. The 'bull wheel' (in the top right of the photograph) drives the cable of the lift. The gondolas are attached to the cable by spring-loaded grips, which detach when the gondolas enter the station. Here, the cabins move slowly, allowing passengers to disembark. The photograph clearly shows the track along which the cabins move, driven by a belt of small rotating tyres. As the gondolas leave the station, they are re-attached to the cable and are accelerated to a speed of up to six metres per second.

Discussing the photographs

▶ List the physical and the human features in these photographs. Sort them into familiar and unfamiliar features in comparison to the school locality.

▶ Talk about the function of the lift system in the images. Can the children describe how it works?

▶ In 'Gondola leaving base', point out the Wilder Kaiser mountains in the background. Ask the children why they think there are no lifts ascending these peaks.

▶ In 'Gondola on mountain', point out the windsock and the anemometer on top of the supporting tower. Why would it be important for the lift operator to measure wind speed and direction? (In high winds, it would be too dangerous for the lift to operate.)

▶ In 'Gondola station', point out the 'bull wheel' and the track which carries the gondola through the lift station. Ask the children to estimate how many people are carried in a cabin (four).

Activities

▶ Use these photographs with the 'Alpine cows' and 'Alms' resources. Ask the children to make a list of all the things that they would see if they were travelling up a Tyrolean mountainside.

▶ One of the main manufacturers of lift systems is an Austrian company, called Doppelmayr. The Hoch Söll/Hohe Salve gondola is an example of a Doppelmayr lift. Get the children to use the company's website (www.doppelmayr.com) to find out about different types of lift systems and to locate on a world map where Doppelmayr lifts have been installed.

▶ Challenge the children to construct a simple powered-lift system to carry a load up a slope. They could use a pulley system or devise different methods of transportation.

Gondola in winter

This photograph shows a gondola lift at work in winter, carrying skiers up a mountain. Söll is at the centre of the 'SkiWelt' (Ski World) region of the Tyrol, which has 93 lifts and 250km of ski runs or 'pistes', spread around nine resorts. The main disadvantage of this region is that it lies at a relatively low level compared with other ski areas, so resorts sometimes have to use artificial snow machines to maintain the pistes.

Skis have been used as transport in Alpine countries for thousands of years. The solid wood construction of early skis has been superseded by carbon fibre, metal and plastic and skis are now highly manoeuvrable and light.

Discussing the photograph

▶ List the physical and human features in the picture.

▶ Ask the children to identify the season of the year.

▶ Talk about skiing. Why do people ski? Point out that, as well as being used for recreation, skis are an everyday form of transport during winters in the Tyrol.

▶ Compare the image of the gondola lift here to the images shown in 'Gondola leaving base' and 'Gondola on mountain'. Apart from the season, are there any other ways in which the lifts appear to be different?

A EUROPEAN LOCALITY: THE TYROL

Activities
▶ Ask the children to make a chart contrasting the different functions of the lifts in winter and summer.
▶ Ski lifts and skiing have a significant impact on mountain landscapes throughout the year. Discuss the possible advantages and disadvantages of turning a mountain village into a ski resort. (Economic benefits may be outweighed by environmental damage.)
▶ Use the internet or ski holiday brochures to locate the most popular ski resorts in Europe. How many are in the Alps? How many are in other parts of Europe? Which resort is the highest? Where are the ski areas in other parts of the world?

A TYROLEAN VILLAGE IN SUMMER

Söll in summer

This photograph shows Söll (pronounced 'surl') in summer. It shows a typical Tyrolean 'onion-domed' church, a hotel and a gift shop. In the background, forested mountains can be seen. Söll lies in the broad Sollandl valley with the jagged, limestone peaks of the Wilder Kaiser mountains to the north and the more rounded peak of the Hohe Salve to the south.

The maypole is a symbol of the 'Dorf fest', one of many village festivals that take place during the year. On 1 May, the pole – which is made from a single tree – is erected and objects are hung from the branches and garlands at the top. Young men of the village are challenged to climb up the pole and retrieve the objects.

The most important festival in Söll is the 'Almabtrieb' in September when the cows are brought down from their mountain pastures to farms in the valley. The cows are decorated with garlands and are led in procession through the village by the local brass band. The festivals have a dual purpose of maintaining local culture and attracting tourists almost every weekend in the summer.

Street in Söll

This photograph shows the main pedestrian area in the centre of Söll. Hotels, shops and a bank can be seen. Like many Tyrolean villages, Söll has changed considerably in the past 50 years. The village's main function as a settlement has changed from serving the agricultural community to meeting the needs of tourists. The resident population of the village stands at around 3500 but there are now approximately 4000 beds for visitors. Since 1959, when the ski lift to the top of Hohe Salve Mountain opened, Söll has attracted many thousands of skiers every winter. It is also a successful summer resort. There is a programme of activities for children and a large swimming pool with slides, sprayers and an artificial waterfall. The hospitality industry offers the main employment in Söll, although some residents continue to work in agriculture and forestry.

Primary school in Söll

This is the recently built 'Volksschule' in Söll, which takes children from six- to ten-years-old. Söll also has a 'Hauptschule' (secondary school). This school has an energy-saving design and is large for a village of Söll's size – indicating that it has a large catchment area. Points to note in the picture include: the pond and garden plots for each class in front of the building, the balcony and canopies to shade the classrooms and the external staircase. Not apparent in the picture, but worthy of note, are the lack of a hard-surfaced playground outside the school, the large internal sports hall and, compared to many UK primary schools, the rather formal layout of the classrooms – all the children have individual desks set out in rows facing the front of the room. More photographs of the school can be seen at the school's website – www.vs-soell.tsn.at. (From the site, click on 'Fotos'.)

Discussing the photographs
▶ Compare the buildings in the pictures to local buildings. Ask the children how we know that the large building in the background of 'Söll in summer' is a church.
▶ Compare the school in Söll to your school. How is it similar/different?
▶ Point out the extensive use of wood in the buildings and the decorated pole in 'Söll in

summer'. Does the forested mountain in the background give a clue to why wood is used so much?
▶ Ask the children if they know of any traditional festivals like the 'Dorf fest' in their locality or in the UK as a whole. Make links to May Day events and Harvest festivals, which are similar to the 'Almabtrieb' in Söll.

Activities
▶ Ask the children to list all of the features they recognise in 'Söll in summer' and 'Street in Söll' and sort them into physical and human features. Sort the human features into familiar and unfamiliar ones in comparison to the school locality.
▶ Locate Söll on the map of the Tyrol (provided on the CD). Note its position in relation to other settlements such as Innsbruck and to physical features such as the Wilder Kaiser mountains.
▶ Ask the children to design posters advertising Söll as a tourist destination in summer and in winter.
▶ Set up a role-play scenario in which a business person wants to build a factory making wooden furniture on the edge of the village. The factory will be quite large and employ at least 50 people. Once trained, skilled workers will be well paid and work shorter hours than in local hotels. What would different people and interest groups in the village think about this? Working in small groups, the children should prepare a case for a planning meeting. Roles could include: a hotel owner; someone who works long hours in a hotel kitchen; a forestry worker; a local tourist-board worker; a worker for a ski lift company; a member of the local fire brigade who is also in the village band. The people in the village would take a range of points of view; they might be in favour of the development because it would diversify employment or opposed to it because it would make the village less attractive to tourists.

Grossglockner and glacier

This image shows the Grossglockner (meaning 'big bell'), Austria's highest mountain at 3797 metres. In the valley at the foot of the mountain is the Pasterze Glacier – an eight-kilometre long 'river' of ice. Glaciers occur where snowfall in winter exceeds melting in summer. The snow slowly compacts until it turns into solid ice, the weight of which causes the glacier to slowly creep downhill. On the surface, deep cracks and crevasses form, making travel over the glacier very dangerous. The glacier has a distinct blue tint from the tiny air bubbles, caused by repeated freezing and thawing. Glaciers once covered much of Northern Europe during an ice age period that ended only about 10,000 years ago. Glacial features, such as U-shaped valleys and large, bowl-shaped depressions called cirques or cwms are still evident in upland areas of the UK.

This photograph was taken in summer and some evidence of melting can be seen at the fringes of the glacier. Even in summer, this is a harsh landscape with little vegetation and year-round snow on the peaks. The Grossglockner is in the Hohe Tauern National Park on the edge of the Tyrol. It is approached by the Hoch Alpen Strasse (High Mountain Road) – a 50km road which ascends from 800 to 2500m above sea level through a series of over 30 tight hairpin bends. The Hoch Alpen Strasse is a popular tourist destination in summer.

Discussing the photograph
▶ Ask the children if they can see any human features in the picture. Why not?
▶ What physical features can be seen? Point out that the picture was taken in summer. How do we know that the landscape is high in the mountains?
▶ Make a list of words to describe the landscape.
▶ Point out the glacier. Explain that it is a river of ice and how it is formed. What features can the children see on and around the glacier? What do they think the surface of the glacier might be like if they stood on it?

Activities
▶ Ask the children to make a sketch of the scene and to annotate it with appropriate labels. They might label: the Grossglockner, the snow on the peaks, the glacier, crevasses and the U-shaped valley cut by the glacier.
▶ The Hohe Tauern National Park is home to a wide variety of wildlife. Challenge the children to find out how animals such as marmots have adapted to the harsh environment.

A EUROPEAN LOCALITY: THE TYROL

Mountain refuge

This picture shows the Drei Zinnen Hutte, a mountain refuge or lodge, high in the Italian Dolomites at 2406 metres above sea level. The Dolomites are a part of the Alps in the South Tyrol, a province of northern Italy that was part of Austria until 1919. Mountain refuges are isolated settlements, usually consisting of single buildings, built to accommodate walkers and climbers undertaking high-altitude treks. They are places of safety if the weather turns bad and usually offer quite basic facilities. The Drei Zinnen Hutte (or 'Refugio Locatelli' in Italian) is an exception because it has several bedrooms and offers a simple food menu. It is open from late June to late September. Although the picture looks wintry, it shows summer snow – not an unusual phenomenon at this altitude. The 'Drei Zinnen' (three chimneys), from which the refuge takes its name, are three stark, jagged, limestone peaks that are attractive to climbers.

Discussing the photograph
▶ Discuss what physical and human features can be seen in the picture.
▶ Ask the children how the building is similar/different to other Tyrolean buildings that they have seen. What do they think the building is used for?
▶ Ask the children to suggest what time of year the photograph was taken. Explain that, although it looks like winter, the picture was taken during the summer months. At this altitude, all precipitation will be in the form of snow.
▶ Point out the sign on the side of the building. Why is it in two languages? Explain that this part of the Tyrol is now in Italy, but used to be part of Austria. Because of this, it is a bilingual area with both German and Italian recognised as official languages. Signs, such as the one on the side of the refuge, are usually written in both languages.

Activities
▶ Ask the children to make a chart comparing this settlement with one of the farms/alms. They should record similarities and differences, noting in particular differences in the surrounding landscape and building materials.
▶ Ask the children to find out about any parts of the UK where two languages are spoken.

Video: Panorama of Innsbruck

The capital of the Tyrol province is Innsbruck. It lies on the River Inn at the crossroads of several routes, the most important being the Brenner Pass to Italy. Innsbruck played host to the Winter Olympics in 1964 and 1976 and the Bergisel Ski Jump is a distinctive local landmark. The video shows a panoramic view from the Stadtturm (City Tower) in the city centre. Although it does not give a full 360 degree panorama, the view takes in some major landmarks, including the domes of Dom St Jakob (St Jakob's Cathedral). In the background, the Nordkette Mountains can be seen rising above the city. The Stadtturm is 51m high and was built between 1442 and 1450 as a watch tower to guard against fires in the tightly packed streets of the Old Town. The viewing platform is a popular tourist attraction.

Discussing the panorama
▶ Explain that the panorama shows a view from a tall tower in the centre of Innsbruck, the capital of the Tyrol. Slowly move the image so that the children can take in an overall impression of the view. Minimise the view and ask the children to list the features that they have seen, from memory.
▶ Zoom in on the image to show particular features such as the Cathedral and the blocks of flats in the distance. Ask the children what human and physical features they can see. What does the site of Innsbruck appear to be like? Is it on a high mountain or in a valley?
▶ Because Innsbruck is a city, many people live in blocks of flats just outside the city centre. Can the children see any of these residential developments? What types of settlements can be seen on the hillsides above the city? (Farms and hamlets.) Why do the children think the city has not spread out into these hills?

Activities
▶ As a class, brainstorm a list of words to describe the children's impressions of Innsbruck.
▶ Ask the children to imagine that a tall tower has been built on top of the school – how

would the view compare to that from the Stadtturm? Get them to make a chart comparing Innsbruck to the school locality. They should use headings such as buildings, places of worship, physical features, size of settlement.

▶ Choose an appropriate open space in the school grounds. Stand the children in a circle facing outwards and ask them to draw the view immediately in front of them. Once they have done this, gather in the pictures and make a display in the form of a panorama. Label the physical and human features on the panorama and compare it to the view seen from the Stadtturm.

Climate chart: Innsbruck and Manchester

The chart shows precipitation and mean (average) temperatures over a period of one year recorded at the airports at Manchester in the UK and Innsbruck in the Tyrol. Precipitation, referring to both rain and snow fall, is presented in the form of a bar chart. Mean temperature is shown as a line graph. The chart shows that Innsbruck has a continental climate with cold winters and warm summers. In Manchester, the variations in temperature and precipitation over the year are less pronounced – the difference in mean temperatures between the coldest and warmest months is just over 11° Celsius. In Innsbruck the difference is over 22° Celsius.

Discussing the chart

▶ Explain the meaning of the terms 'mean temperature' and 'precipitation'. Ask the children to identify how these are shown on the chart. What does the line show? How is precipitation shown on the chart?

▶ Explain that the precipitation in Innsbruck from November to March/April will be in the form of snow. In Manchester, some precipitation in those months will be in the form of snow but mainly it will be rain. What is the difference between the mean temperatures in Manchester and Innsbruck in December, January and February?

▶ Point out where the freezing point (0°C) falls on the chart. Is there a month in Manchester or Innsbruck when the mean temperature falls below freezing point? (Innsbruck in January.)

▶ Ask the children to identify which place has the climate with the biggest difference between warmest and coldest months.

▶ Discuss the pattern of precipitation during the year in Manchester and Innsbruck. In Manchester, the highest rainfall appears to be in the autumn. In Innsbruck, the months with most rainfall are in the spring and summer. (Much of this rain will come in thundery downpours.)

Activities

▶ Ask the children to use travel planning websites to plan a trip to Innsbruck from Manchester or from your school's local airport. They should identify different possible routes and cost a short stay for a family, including accommodation. Alternatively, they could plan a trip using surface transport such as ferry, Eurotunnel or train.

▶ Ask the children to write a list of items they would include in a small suitcase for weekend trips to Innsbruck or Söll at different times of the year, bearing in mind the climate information on the chart. When would they need warm clothes, waterproofs, sun block?

▶ Use weather information on the Söll Website – www.soell.com – to make a short-term record of weather in the village and in the Tyrol region. The site contains information on temperature and weather conditions that is updated on a daily basis. Compare this weather data to similar data gathered in the school locality. Ask the children to use data handling software on a computer to produce charts comparing weather conditions in the two localities over a week or a month.

Video: Alps from the air

This short movie clip shows an aerial view of the Alps in winter. It is a landscape of jagged peaks and deep snow under a clear blue sky. The impression is one of a timeless, pristine environment on which the presence of people can have little effect. There is growing evidence, however, that climate change is having an impact. Glaciers are retreating and the snow, needed by winter skiers, is becoming short-lived at lower altitudes (see 'Alpine crisis' photocopiable page 80).

A EUROPEAN LOCALITY: THE TYROL

Discussing the video
▶ Before starting the clip, question the children about the landscape they can see on the opening screen. Is this in a valley or high in the mountains? How would they describe the scene?
▶ Explain that this short film has been taken by a camera in an aeroplane or helicopter flying over part of the Alps. The camera will rise over the rocky ridge seen on the first screen. Ask the children to predict what they think the landscape will be like on the other side.
▶ After showing the clip, ask the children to describe the scene on the far side of the ridge.

Activities
▶ As a class, brainstorm a list of words to describe the landscape in the high Alps in winter.
▶ Discuss the issue of developments in unspoiled landscapes, such as this. Explain that high mountain areas are under threat from skiing-based developments. Discuss the pros and cons of developing ski resorts.

NOTES ON THE PHOTOCOPIABLE PAGES

Word cards — PAGES 78–79

These cards contain some of the basic and more advanced vocabulary for the children to learn and use when looking at localities in the Tyrol. They include:
▶ names of settlements
▶ vocabulary associated with mountains and work and leisure in the mountains.

Read through the word cards with the children to familiarise them with the key words of the unit. Ask which words the children have heard before and clarify any that they don't understand.

Activities
▶ Shuffle the cards and spread out a set of cards on each group's table. Ask the children to find specific words you call out.
▶ Use the cards as a word bank to help the children label pictures and to help them with longer pieces of writing.
▶ Begin a glossary with the words and include any other topic vocabulary used in the unit.
▶ Make a display in the form of a concept map with arrows linking the cards to show definitions and links. By the end of the unit, the display should provide a lively visual record of the places, geographical terms and concepts that have been encountered.

'Alpine crisis' newspaper article — PAGE 80

There is now great pressure from business people in the skiing industry to build facilities and resorts at higher altitudes where snow appears to be guaranteed. Environmental campaigners and organisations, such as the International Commission for the Protection of the Alps (www.cipra.org), are deeply opposed to these developments. This newspaper article outlines the pressures on the Alpine skiing industry, its response and the views of business people, skiers and activists.

Discussing the text
▶ Discuss what features of journalistic writing the article shows. How does the writer get the reader's attention? Is there evidence of bias?
▶ Ask the children what questions they would ask the people interviewed in the article.

Activities
▶ Ask the children to write a script or improvise a television or radio interview with either a ski resort promoter or a green campaigner. What questions would the interviewer ask? What replies would the two interviewees give? The business person would probably stress the importance of skiing to the Tyrol and maintaining employment. The campaigner would object to the defacement of the landscape and the increased pollution.
▶ Challenge the children to make a poster or design a simple website advocating one of the points of view.

Tyrol word cards

A EUROPEAN LOCALITY: THE TYROL

Alps
Austria
Tyrol
Söll
Innsbruck
Grossglockner
mountain
glacier

Tyrol word cards

A EUROPEAN LOCALITY: THE TYROL

| alm |
| cable lift |
| gondola |
| cattle |
| hay |
| skiing |
| Dorf fest |
| Volksschule |

'Alpine crisis' newspaper article

A EUROPEAN LOCALITY: THE TYROL

Fight to the last resort as Alpine crisis looms

Robin McKie

Europe's winter playground, a region of mighty peaks and stunning scenery, has been visited by millions every year. But, with climate change taking a grip, the Alps are set to become a battleground between developers and conservationists.

On one side, businessmen are preparing to build new ski resorts among the highest peaks and glaciers. They say global warming poses such a threat that they can only save the sport by going upwards. Their plans include resorts in Austria at above 3350 metres.

On the other side stand the green activists, annoyed by what they see as an attack on the Alps' last natural, pristine habitats. They have promised to fight the developers to the last.

The battle promises to be bitter, although both sides do agree about the cause – global warming. Many of the Alps' most popular resorts lie at relatively low levels and are in danger of running out of snow as the world warms up.

A recent report, by the United Nations, said that in 30 years the snowline in the Alps will rise by 300m. Resorts in some areas of Austria will simply dry up. Other areas will suffer avalanches, landslips and floods. A half of all resorts in Europe may have to close within the next 50 years.

This prospect is now causing serious alarm among Alpine nations, which fear they could lose billions. Millions visit the Alps in winter and hundreds of thousands depend on the sport for their living.

Politicians throughout the Alps are now being pressed to relax environmental rules that might block new developments. This applies in particular to the higher, colder, parts of the Alps. Earlier this year, the government of the Tyrol lifted bans on building of ski lifts in high regions and on glaciers.

Developers are preparing to build two major projects. One, at Kaunertal, would open up the second largest glacier in the eastern Alps, and allow tourists to ski at more than 3500m. The second would include building cable cars at Fernerkogel. Again, previously undeveloped land would be opened up for tourism.

The prospect of these developments upsets environmental groups. 'It is just the wrong way to tackle this issue,' said Michel Revaz, of the International Commission for the Protection of the Alps. 'These glaciers are the last pure places in the Alps. They should not be polluted with fuel, and oil, and debris.' Conservationists want other forms of tourism – such as hiking, sledding and climbing – to be promoted in resorts.

Abridged version from *The Observer*, 19 September 2004.